Test Prep Works, LLC,
PROVIDES A NEW APPROACH TO MATERIALS

Are you an education professional?

You know your students. You know the test.
Shouldn't your materials reflect that?

The Test Prep Works advantages include:

- A low, one-time set up fee with no minimum purchases
- Buy only the books that you need, when you need them
- Access to the Test Prep Works tutoring forum where you can exchange ideas with other tutors and request additional materials

TEST PREP WORKS

CAN PROVIDE MATERIALS FOR YOUR SCHOOL OR TUTORING COMPANY. WE OFFER THE ABILITY TO CUSTOMIZE OUR MATERIALS TO REFLECT THE IDENTITY OF YOUR SCHOOL OR COMPANY.

Please visit www.TestPrepWorks.com for more information

Strategies proven to work.

Content Instruction created just for the Middle Level SSAT. Practice to reinforce learning.

✓ Strategies for each of the different sections

✓ Content instruction gives you just what you need for the Middle Level SSAT

✓ Drills and Practice Sets that make the difference on test day

✓ Expert advice for the newly updated (2012) writing sample

SUCCESS

ON THE Middle Level SSAT

A Complete Course

Christa Abbott, M.Ed.

Published by:
Test Prep Works, LLC
741 N. Danville St.
Arlington, VA 22201
www.TestPrepWorks.com

SSAT is a registered trademark of the Secondary School Admission Test Board. They have not endorsed nor are they associated with this book.

Neither the author nor the publisher of this book claims responsibility for the accuracy of this book or the outcome of students who use these materials.

ISBN: 978-1-939090-02-7

Contents

Percent Problems

Average Problems

Solving Equations

Word Problems

Geometry

About the Author

Christa Abbott has been a private test prep tutor for over a decade. She has worked with students who have been admitted to and attended some of the top independent schools in the country. Over the years, she has developed materials for each test that truly make the difference.

Christa is a graduate of Middlebury College and received her Masters in Education from the University of Virginia, a program nationally known for its excellence. Her background in education allows her to develop materials based on the latest research about how we learn so that preparation can be an effective and efficient use of time. Her materials are also designed to be developmentally appropriate for the ages of the students taking the tests. In her free time, she enjoys hiking, tennis, Scrabble, and reading. Her greatest joy is spending time with her husband and three children.

Christa continues to work with students one-on-one in the Washington, D.C., area. She also works with students internationally via Skype. If you are interested in these services, please visit www.ChristaAbbott.com.

About Test Prep Works, LLC

Test Prep Works, LLC, was founded to provide effective materials for test preparation. Its founder, Christa Abbott, spent years looking for effective materials for the private school entrance exams but came up empty-handed. The books  available combined several different tests and while there are overlaps, they are not the same test. Christa found this to be very, very overwhelming for students who were in Elementary and Middle School and that just didn't seem necessary. Christa developed her own materials to use with students that are specific for each level of the test and are not just adapted from other books. For the first time, these materials are available to the general public as well as other tutors. Please visit www.TestPrepWorks.com to view a complete array of offerings as well as sign up for a newsletter with recent news and developments in the world of admissions and test preparation.

Notes for Parents

What is the SSAT?

SSAT stands for Secondary School Admission Test. It is used by many of the top independent schools in the United States. You may have heard of another test, the ISEE (Independent School Entrance Exam). The schools that your student is applying to may accept either the SSAT or the ISEE, or they may exclusively use one test or the other. It can also depend upon what grade your child is applying for. Contact each school that your child will apply to in order to be sure that he or she is taking the correct test.

- Contact schools so that your child takes the right test

What level should I register my child for?

This book is designed to help students who are taking the Middle Level SSAT. If students are currently in grades 5-7, applying for grades 6-8, then they should be taking the Middle Level SSAT.

- Middle Level is for students currently in grades 5-7, applying for grades 6-8

Just how important is the SSAT to the admissions process?

Every school uses the test differently. In general, the more competitive the school, the more test scores are going to matter, but there are certainly exceptions to that rule. Reading through a school's literature is a great way to figure out whether or not a school emphasizes or deemphasizes testing. Also, call the admissions office where your child will be applying. Admissions officers are often quite candid about what the testing profile of their admitted students tends to be.

- Talk to the schools that your child is applying to in order to get a sense of the scores they look for

How can I help my student?

Keep your own cool. Never once has a student gotten a higher score because mom or dad freaked out. Approach this as a project. Good test taking skills can be learned and by working through the process with your child in a constructive manner, you are providing them with a roadmap for how to approach challenges in the future. We want them to be confident, but to earn that confidence through analysis, self-monitoring, and practice.

- Keep a positive attitude

What are the key elements of successful test preparation?

Analysis

It is important that students don't just do practice problem after practice problem without figuring out what they missed, and most importantly WHY they missed those problems. Is there a particular type of problem that they keep missing? One issue that many students have is categorizing problems. When you go through a problem that they are stuck on, be sure to point out the words in the problem that pointed you in the correct direction.

- Teach your child to analyze why he or she missed a question

Self-monitoring

Students should develop a sense of their strengths and weaknesses so that they can best focus preparation time. This book provides many practice opportunities for each section, but your child may not need that. For example, if they are acing the average problems, they shouldn't keep spending valuable time doing more of those problems. Maybe their time would be better spent on vocabulary. This is a great opportunity, and your student is at the perfect age, to be learning how to prioritize.

- Help your student prioritize material to work on

Practice

While it is important that a student understand WHY he is doing what he is doing, at a certain point it just needs to become automatic. This is a timed test and you want the strategies to spring to mind without having to reinvent the wheel every time. Practice will make this process fast and easy. On test day all that practice will kick in to make this a positive and affirming experience for your student.

- Teach your child that he or she needs to practice what they have learned so that it is automatic on test day

What is new for the 2012-2013 testing season?

Please, please be aware that changes are being made to the SSAT. Test Prep Works uses on demand publishing so that our books can be updated as changes are made to the test, but you may have other resources that are not updated.

One big change for the Middle Level SSAT is that it is now called the Middle Level SSAT. Previously, it was called the Lower Level SSAT. In 2012, the SSATB piloted an Elementary Level SSAT, so they renamed the Lower Level SSAT as the Middle Level SSAT to avoid confusion. Another big change was the writing sample. The writing prompts have changed. Previously, students were given a statement that they had to agree or disagree with. Those old prompts have been scrapped and in their place are two fiction writing prompts that students can choose between. They look like "story starters" that your child may have done in school. Each prompt is the starting sentence to a story and students choose which story they would like to complete.

- Students will now choose between two fiction writing prompts that are starting sentences for a story

Please also be aware that the scoring may change on the Middle Level SSAT, possibly as soon as the 2013-2014 school year. As of right now (fall 2012), if a student answers a question and gets it wrong, then they lose a quarter point. At some point in the near future, the SSATB is going to change this so that only the number of questions correct will determine a student's score. Please check on www.TestPrepWorks.com to be kept up to date. You can also look on www.ssat.org, but some of the information is a little harder to find although it is all there.

What do parents need to know about registering their child?

Registration is done through the SSATB. Their website is www.ssat.org. When you register for the test, be sure to also order the official SSATB book, *Preparing and Applying Guide for Independent School Admission and the SSAT.* Nothing can replace the practice tests in this book because they are written by the people who will write the actual test that your student will be taking. One thing to be aware of is that the SSATB released a new version in September of 2012. As of the writing of this book, there are errors in this new practice book. Hopefully, they will be fixed soon. Just know that if you strongly disagree with the answer choice given, you may be right. The book is still a valuable resource to see question types and hopefully the errors will be fixed by the time you order the book!

- Order the practice book from www.SSAT.org
- You may find an error in the official practice book

There are a few other things you should know about registration options:

You can choose from either a national test date or a flex test date.

On the national test dates, the SSAT is given in a group setting. It is a similar experience to what you might remember when you took the SAT. The flex test can be given in the office of an educational consultant in a small group, or even a one-on-one, setting.

There are many advantages of the flex testing.

You can generally pick a day and time. If your child doesn't do well in the morning, schedule it for the afternoon. If you really want to get the test out of the way before the holidays and are away when the national test is given in December, then you can choose another day. Also, fewer students means fewer distractions. Flex testing is more expensive than national testing, but given the investment that you are making in independent school, it can be well worth it. To find consultants in your area, visit www.SSAT.org, click on the "Taking the SSAT" button, and under "Test Information (Middle and Upper Level)", click on "Educational Consultants". (This information is current as of September 2012, but please keep in mind that the SSAT may have changed their website if you cannot find these links).

One big disadvantage of the flex testing is that you can only do it once per testing (or academic) year.

The SSATB only comes up with one form a year for the flex test, so a student can only do flex once each year. They can do flex testing and then one of the national dates if they want to retake the test (or vice versa), however.

The SSATB does offer score choice.

What this means is that you can take the test as many times as you want and then choose the test date (or dates) that you wish to send. Don't stress your student out by having him or her take the test a bunch of times, but for some students it reduces stress to know that they can have another shot at the test.

You must request accommodations if your child needs them.

If your child has an IEP or receives accommodations in school, then start the paperwork with the SSAT board promptly. Don't wait until the last minute as this is very stress inducing for both you and your student. If your child is going to get extended time, he or she should know that as he or she works through practice tests.

Above all else, remember that your student will look to you to see how you approach this challenge. If you become anxious, they will too. If you are confident about developing a game plan and building confidence through practice, this experience will stay with them in a profoundly positive way.

How To Use This Book

This book is designed to teach you what you need to know in order to maximize your Middle Level SSAT performance.

There are strategies for each of the four multiple-choice sections as well as advice on the writing section. This book also includes a lot of content practice. There is a complete vocabulary section and detailed instruction for the math concepts that are tested on the SSAT.

You may find that you don't need to complete all of the content instruction. It is important to prioritize your time! If vocabulary is a weakness for you, then spend your time working through the vocabulary lessons. If some of the math concepts are challenging, then you should spend your study time working through the math sections.

Full practice exams are not included because these are available from the people who actually write the test, the SSAT Board. If you have not already, be sure to go to www.SSAT.org and order *Preparing and Applying Guide for Independent School Admission and the SSAT*. Any time you are studying for a test, the best source of a full practice test is the people who are going to write the test you will be taking. There are two practice tests in *Preparing and Applying for Independent School*.

I have spent years studying the test and analyzing the different question types, content, and the types of answers that the test writers prefer. Now you can benefit from my hard work! I will show how to approach questions so that you can raise your score significantly.

Let's get started!

The Format of the Middle Level SSAT

You can expect to see four scored sections *plus* a writing sample *plus* an experimental section on the Middle Level SSAT.

The four scored sections are:

- ✓ Quantitative (there will be two of these sections on your test)
  - A variety of math problems
  - Each section has 25 problems, for a total of 50 math problems
  - 30 minutes to complete each section, or a little more than a minute per problem

- ✓ Verbal
  - 30 synonym questions and 30 analogy questions
  - 30 minutes to complete the section, or about 30 seconds per question

- ✓ Reading Comprehension
  - Passages and questions
  - Passages can be fiction, non-fiction, and poetry
  - A total of 40 questions
  - Generally 6-8 passages, each passage having 4-8 questions, but this is not carved in stone so you may see some variation
  - 40 minutes to complete section

The four above sections are all multiple choice. Each question has five answer choices.

There are also two other sections that you will see on the SSAT:

The Experimental Section

✓ This was new for the fall of 2012; it is supposed to be 15 minutes long and will NOT contribute to your score

✓ SSATB is just trying out new problems for future tests, not to worry

✓ You may not even see this section (if you have extended time, you probably will not)

The Writing Sample

✓ Will NOT be scored, but a copy will be sent to all of the schools that you apply to

✓ In the summer of 2012, the SSATB changed the format of the writing section - you will now be able to choose one of two writing prompts, both are the beginning sentence of a story and you can choose which story you wish to finish

✓ 25 minutes to write and you will be given two pages to write on

Now, on to the strategies and content! The strategies covered in this book will focus on the multiple-choice sections since those are what is used to determine your percentile. Please also see the essay section for tips on the writing sample.

What Students Need To Know For the SSAT- Just the Basics

Here is what you really need to know to do well on the Middle Level SSAT:

How the Scoring Works

On the Middle Level SSAT, if you get a question correct, then you are given one point. If you answer a question and get it wrong, then they subtract a quarter point. If you don't answer a question at all, then you don't get a point added to your raw score, but they don't take off a quarter point, either.

- If you answer a question correctly, you get one point
- If you answer a question incorrectly, you lose ¼ a point
- If you don't answer the question at all, you don't get a point but you don't lose a ¼ point either

You might be asking why they use this crazy system. The thinking behind it is that on a regular test, you would get ahead by guessing. You would get some of the questions that you guessed on correct and therefore your score would be higher for blindly guessing. Actually, chances are you would get 1/5 of the questions correct if you blindly guessed because there are five answer choices for each question. By taking off a quart point for the 4/5 of the questions that you missed, the test writers are just making sure that you don't get ahead for guessing.

- Ex: You guess on five questions.

  1 correct answer $\times$ 1 = +1 point

  4 incorrect answers $\times -\frac{1}{4} = -1$ point

  _____

  0 points gained or lost

If you think this sounds way too complicated, the SSATB (the people who publish the test) agree. As of the writing of this book (fall 2012), this scoring system is still in place. However, they will be working on phasing it out. As early as 2013 they might not be taking off a quarter point if you get a question wrong. Please, please, please check www.testprepworks.com or www.ssat.org to confirm how the scoring will work. This book will be updated when the change is made, but you may be working with an older copy.

When To Guess

As long as the above scoring policy is in place, you should only guess if you can rule out one answer choice. Once the policy changes, you should answer everything, even if you haven't looked at the question.

What Schools Are Really Looking For and the Beauty of the Percentile Score

You will get a raw score for the SSAT based upon how many you get right or wrong. This raw score will then be converted into a scaled score. Neither of these scores are what schools are really looking at. They are looking for your percentile scores, and in particular the percentile scores that compare you to other students applying to independent school.

Percentile score is what schools are really looking at

The percentile score compares you to other students of the same gender that are in your grade. For example, let's say that you are an eighth grade boy and you scored in the 70th percentile. What this means is that out of a hundred boys in your grade, you would have done better than 70 of them.

Keep in mind that the Middle Level SSAT is given to students through the 7th grade. That means that if you are taking the test in 5th grade, there could very well be some material on the test that you simply have not yet covered. You may miss some of these questions, but as long as the other students your age also miss them, then it won't affect your percentile score.

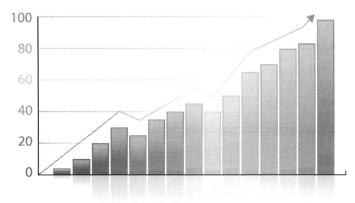

Your percentile score compares you only to other students in your grade

Many students applying to independent schools are used to getting almost all the questions correct on a test. You will probably miss more questions on this test than you are used to missing, but because the percentile score is what schools are looking at, don't let it get to you.

You may miss more questions than you are used to, but that is OK as long as other students your age miss those questions

You should also look at the scoring chart in *Preparing and Applying for Independent School*. On the quantitative section, if you scored a 40 out of 50 (this assumes that you got 80% of the questions correct and did not answer the others), you would score in around the 80th percentile. In school if you got an 80% on a test, you might not be pleased. But to score in the 80th percentile on the SSAT would put you in the running for just about any school in America.

Also keep in mind that the charts in *Preparing and Applying for Independent School* do NOT take into account different grade levels but your actual scores will. If you are in fifth grade, your percentile scores will be higher. For example, I recently had two fifth-grade students who both scored 30 out of 40 on the reading section. They missed ¼ of the questions, but they both still scored in the 99th percentile (this is the highest possible score). My point here is that you shouldn't get discouraged if you are on the younger end of the age range and it feels like you are getting a lot of questions wrong. As long as the other students your age are struggling as well, you can still get a fantastic percentile score.

The Mother of All Strategies

Use Ruling Out

If you remember nothing else on test day, remember to use process of elimination. This is a multiple-choice test, and there are often answers that don't even make sense.

When you read a question, you want to read all of the answer choices before selecting one. You need to keep in mind that the test will ask you to choose the answer choice that "best" answers the question. Best is a relative word, so how can you know which answer choice best answers the question if you don't read them all?

- After you read the question, read ALL of the answer choices
- Look for the "best" answer, which may just be the least wrong answer choice

After you have read all of the answer choices, rule them out in order from most wrong to least wrong. Sometimes the "best" answer choice is not a great fit, but it is better than the others. This process will also clarify your thinking so that by the time you get down to only two answer choices, you have a better idea of what makes choices right or wrong.

- Rule out in order from most wrong to least wrong

Above all else, remember that you are playing the odds on this test. To increase your score, you need to answer questions even when you are not positive of the answer.

Let's say that you rule out three answer choices on four questions. You then guess on those questions. If you get two of those questions correct (which is the most likely outcome), then the scoring would look like this:

$$2 \text{ questions correct} \times 1 \text{ point each} = +2 \text{ points}$$
$$2 \text{ questions incorrect} \times -\frac{1}{4} \text{ point each} = -\frac{1}{2} \text{ point}$$

$$\text{total change to score} = +1\frac{1}{2} \text{ points}$$

Now let's say that you only get 1 question correct out of those 4 questions. The scoring would look like this:

$$1 \text{ question correct} \times 1 \text{ point each} = +1 \text{ point}$$
$$3 \text{ questions incorrect} \times -\frac{1}{4} \text{ point each} = -\frac{3}{4} \text{ point}$$
$$\text{total change to score} = +\frac{1}{4} \text{ point}$$

As you can see, if you missed 3 questions and only answered one question correctly, you would still come out ahead.

- Ruling out allows you to play the odds- and that is how you will come out ahead of your peers

Verbal section– Basic strategies

In the verbal section you will see two question types:

- Synonyms
- Analogies

On the synonym questions, you will be given one question word and then you have to choose the answer choice that has the word that comes closest in meaning to the question word.

Synonym questions look something like this:

1. JOYOUS
   (A) loud
   (B) crying
   (C) happy
   (D) shy
   (E) lame

Out of all the answer choice words, happy comes closest in meaning to joyous. Choice C is correct.

The synonyms questions probably won't be quite this easy, but you get the idea.

The analogies questions generally give you two words and you have to figure out the relationship between them and then choose the answer choice that has the same relationship.

The analogy questions usually look something like this:

1. Panther is to cat as
   (A) lion is to jungle
   (B) wolf is to dog
   (C) chick is to bluejay
   (D) mouse is to guinea pig
   (E) horse is to cow

In this case, a panther is a wild cat. A wolf is a wild dog, so choice B is correct.

Sometimes, you will be given the first word in the answer relationship and you just have to choose the second word.

These questions look like this:

1. Tall is to short as narrow is to
   (A) long
   (B) square
   (C) wide
   (D) measured
   (E) lax

Tall and short are opposites, so we are looking for the answer choice that is the opposite of narrow. Wide is the opposite of narrow, so choice C is correct.

Since synonym and analogy questions are very different, we use different strategies for them.

Synonym strategies

There are several strategies that we can use on the synonyms section. Which strategy you use for an individual question is highly variable. It depends on what roots you know, whether or not you have heard the word before, and your gut sense about a word.

Think of these strategies as being your toolbox. Several tools can get the job done.

One thing that you should note is that the synonym questions tend to go in order from easiest to most difficult. The difficulty of the question will affect which strategy you use.

Here are the strategies:

- Come up with your own word
- Is it positive or negative?
- Can you think of a sentence or phrase in which you have heard the word?
- Are there any roots or word parts that you recognize?
- If you have to guess, see if there is an answer choice that has the same prefix, suffix or root as the question word

Strategy #1: Come up with your own word

Use this strategy when you read through a sentence and a word just pops into your head. Don't force yourself to try to come up with your own definition when you aren't sure what the word means.

- Use this strategy when definition pops into your head

If you read a question word and a synonym pops into your head, go ahead and jot it down. It is important that you write down the word because otherwise you may try to talk yourself into an answer choice that "seems to come close". One of the biggest enemies on any standardized test is doubt. Doubt leads to talking yourself into the wrong answer, and physically writing down the word gives you the confidence you need when you go through the answer choices.

- Physically write down the definition- don't hold it in your head

After you write down the word, start by crossing out answer choices that are not synonyms for your word. By the time you get down to two choices, you will have a much better idea of what you are looking for.

- Cross out words that don't work

The following drill contains words that you may be able think of a definition for. These are the types of words that you are likely to see at the beginning of the synonym section. You should focus on creating good habits with these questions.

What are good habits?

- Jot down the definition- this will actually save time in the long run
- Use ruling out- physically cross out answer choices that you know are incorrect

Drill #1

1. RAPID:
   (A) marvelous
   (B) exhausted
   (C) swift
   (D) professional
   (E) icy

2. STEADY
   (A) constant
   (B) nervous
   (C) friendly
   (D) hollow
   (E) cozy

3. DEBRIS
   (A) whim
   (B) trash
   (C) core
   (D) knapsack
   (E) humor

4. PLAYFUL
   (A) loud
   (B) careful
   (C) honest
   (D) fun
   (E) respectful

5. SEQUENCE
   (A) nation
   (B) resource
   (C) bid
   (D) farce
   (E) order

(Answers to drills are found at the end of the verbal strategies section)

Strategy #2: Using positive or negative

Sometimes you see a word, and you couldn't define that word, but you have a "gut feeling" that it is either something good or something bad. Maybe you don't know what that word means, but you know you would be mad if someone called you that!

- You have to have a gut feeling about a word to use this strategy

To use this strategy, when you get that feeling that a word is either positive or negative, then write in a + or a – sign next to the word. Then go to your answer choices and rule out anything that is opposite, i.e., positive when your question word is negative or negative when your question word is positive.

- Physically write a + or – sign after the question word

To really make this strategy work for you, you also need to rule out any words that are neutral, or neither positive nor negative. For example, let's say the question word is DISTRESS. Distress is clearly a negative word. So we could rule out a positive answer choice, such as friendly, but we can also rule out a neutral word, such as sleepy. At night, it is good to be sleepy, during the day it is not. Sleepy is not clearly a negative word, so it goes.

- Rule out words that are opposite from your question word
- Also rule out neutral words

To summarize, here are the basic steps to using this strategy:

1. If you have a gut negative or positive feeling about a word, write a + or – sign next to the question word
2. Rule out any words that are opposite
3. Also rule out any NEUTRAL words
4. Pick from what is left

Here is an example of a question where you may be able to use the positive/negative strategy:

1. CONDEMN:
   (A) arrive
   (B) blame
   (C) tint
   (D) favor
   (E) laugh

Let's say that you know that condemn is bad, but you can't think of a definition. We write a – sign next to it and then rule out anything that is positive. That means that choices D and E can go because they are both positive. Now we can also rule out neutral words because we know condemn has to be negative. Arrive and tint are neither positive nor negative, so choices A and C are out. We are left with choice B, which is correct.

On the following drill, write a + or – sign next to each question word. Then rule out answer choices that are opposite or neutral. Pick from what is left. Even if you aren't sure if the question word is positive or negative, take a guess at it! You may get more right than you would have imagined.

1. ALLURE
   (A) attraction
   (B) color
   (C) disgrace
   (D) wilderness
   (E) confidence

2. SERENE
   (A) confusing
   (B) musical
   (C) dark
   (D) tall
   (E) calm

3. HUMANE
   (A) invalid
   (B) compassionate
   (C) portable
   (D) restricted
   (E) bashful

4. DEJECTED
   (A) resourceful
   (B) humid
   (C) depressed
   (D) proper
   (E) cheery

5. REEK
   (A) express
   (B) qualify
   (C) thrill
   (D) stink
   (E) flavor

(Answers to drills are found at the end of the verbal strategies section)

Strategy #3: Use context - Think of where you have heard the word before

Use this strategy when you can't define a word, but you can think of a sentence or phrase where you have heard the word before.

- This strategy only works when you have heard the word before

To apply this strategy, think of a sentence or phrase where you have heard the question word before. Then try plugging the answer choices into your phrase to see which one has the same meaning within that sentence or phrase.

- Think of a sentence or phrase where you have heard the word before
- Plug question words into that sentence or phrase

Here is an example:

1. SHIRK
    (A) rush
    (B) send
    (C) learn
    (D) avoid
    (E) clutter

Now let's say you have heard the word "shirk" but can't define it. You remember your mom telling you "don't shirk your responsibilities" when you tried to watch TV before your chores were done. So we plug in the answer choices for the word shirk in your sentence. Does it make sense to say "don't rush your responsibilities"? It might make sense, but it wouldn't have the same meaning as your context. You weren't in trouble for rushing your chores, you were in trouble for not doing them at all so we can rule out choice A. Does it make sense to say "don't send your responsibilities"? Not at all. Choice B is out. Does "don't learn your responsibilities" work? Nope, choice C is out. Would your mom say "don't avoid your responsibilities"? You bet. Choice D is correct. We would also plug in choice E to make sure it wasn't a better fit, but in this case it is not and choice D is correct.

Sometimes the only word or phrase that you can think of uses a different form of the word. That is OK as long as you change the answer choices when you plug them in.

- You can use a different form of the word, just change answer choices as well

Here is an example:

1. CHERISH:
    (A) treasure
    (B) enforce
    (C) utter
    (D) concern
    (E) calm

Maybe you have heard your English teacher talk about *Little Women* as "one of my most cherished books." We can use that context, we just have to add the –ed to the answer choices when we plug them in. Does it make sense to say "one of my most treasured books"? Yes, it does, so we will keep choice A. Would "one of my most enforced books" work? No, so we can rule out choice B. What about "one of my most uttered books" or "one of my most concerned books" or "one of my most calmed books"? No, no, and no, so we rule out choices C, D, and E. Choice A is correct.

In the following drill, if you have heard the word before, then come up with a sentence or phrase and practice our strategy. If you have not heard the word before, you can't use the strategy of thinking where you have heard the word before! Use another strategy and ruling out to answer the question anyways. You may not get every question correct, but remember, nothing ventured, nothing gained.

Drill #3

1. WILY
   (A) serious
   (B) flattering
   (C) tough
   (D) cunning
   (E) powerful

2. PROPHESY
   (A) quiver
   (B) copy
   (C) mystify
   (D) predict
   (E) advance

3. ABOLISH
   (A) end
   (B) salute
   (C) liberate
   (D) manage
   (E) baffle

4. APPALLING
   (A) worthy
   (B) horrifying
   (C) available
   (D) omitted
   (E) various

5. CONSENT
   (A) worry
   (B) knowledge
   (C) approval
   (D) draft
   (E) requirement

(Answers to drills are found at the end of the verbal strategies section)

Strategy #4: Look for roots or word parts that you know

This strategy works when you recognize that a word looks like another word that you know or when you recognize one of the roots that you have studied in school or in this book.

If you see something familiar in the question word, underline the roots or word parts that you recognize. If you can think of the meaning of the root, then look for answer choices that would go with that meaning. If you can't think of a specific meaning, think of other words that have that root and look for answer choices that are similar in meaning to those other words.

- Underline word parts that you recognize
- Think of the meaning of that word part
- If you can't think of a meaning, think of other words with that word part

Here is an example of a question that uses a word with recognizable word parts:

1. EXCLUDE:
    (A) prohibit
    (B) feel
    (C) rest
    (D) drift
    (E) rejoice

There are two word parts in the word "exclude" that can help us out. First, we have the prefix ex-, which means out (think of the word exit). Secondly, clu is a word root that means to shut (think of the word include). Using these word parts, we can see that exclude has something to do with shutting out. Choice A comes closest to this meaning, so it is correct.

For the following drill, try to use word parts to come up with the correct answer choice. If you can't think of what the word root, prefix, or suffix means, then think of other words that have the same root, prefix, or suffix.

Drill #4

1. MAGNANIMOUS
   (A) possible
   (B) generous
   (C) cruel
   (D) restrained
   (E) barren

2. POSTPONE
   (A) allow
   (B) recruit
   (C) delay
   (D) stifle
   (E) label

3. SUBTERRANEAN
   (A) partial
   (B) tragic
   (C) appreciative
   (D) hectic
   (E) underground

4. ERR
   (A) stumble
   (B) fix
   (C) expand
   (D) gasp
   (E) laugh

5. NONDESCRIPT
   (A) wise
   (B) occasional
   (C) dreadful
   (D) vague
   (E) lazy

(Answers to drills are found at the end of the verbal strategies section)

Strategy #5: Guess an answer choice with the same prefix, suffix, or word root as the question word

If nothing else, if you have no idea what the word means but you see an answer choice that has the same root, prefix, or suffix, guess that answer choice! You would be amazed how many correct answers have the same root as the question word. What if there are two answer choices with the same root? Guess one of them. Remember, if we can rule out even one answer choice, we should guess.

Let's look at the following example:

1.   PERMISSIBLE
     (A) edible
     (B) crazy
     (C) strong
     (D) allowable
     (E) gentle

Even if you don't know what permissible means, the –ible ending tells us that it must mean able to do something. The –ible and –able suffixes have the same meaning, so we could guess between choices A and D. Edible means able to be eaten, but allowable is a synonym for permissible, so choice D is correct.

Complete the following drill by looking for answer choices that repeat roots, prefixes, or suffixes.

Drill #5

1. CONGEAL
   (A) bury
   (B) habituate
   (C) coagulate
   (D) reimburse
   (E) limit

2. DISPARAGE
   (A) resurrect
   (B) discredit
   (C) deceive
   (D) praise
   (E) label

3. COMPREHENSIBLE
   (A) laudable
   (B) independent
   (C) remorseful
   (D) authentic
   (E) understandable

(Answers to drills are found at the end of the verbal strategies section)

Now you have the strategies that you need to succeed on the synonyms section! To keep improving your score, keep studying that vocabulary.

Strategies for the Analogies Section

The analogies section tests not only your vocabulary, but also your ability to see how words are related.

We have two main strategies for the analogies section:

- If you know the question words, make a sentence
- If you don't know one of the question words, head to the answer choices

Strategy #1: Make a sentence from the question words

In order to use this strategy, you have to at least have a vague sense of what both question words mean. Basically, you make a sentence from the question words and then plug answer choices into that sentence to see which answer choice has the same relationship.

Here is an example of a question with words that we know and can make a sentence from:

1. Water is to ocean as
   (A) cloud is to sky
   (B) mountain is to hill
   (C) paint is to watercolor
   (D) ice is to glaciers
   (E) sneaker is to marathon

If we make a sentence from the question words, we might say "water fills the ocean". Now we plug in our answer choices, subbing in the answer words for the question words. Does it make sense to say "cloud fills the sky"? Sometimes that is true, but if we have to use the word sometimes, then it is not a strong relationship so we can rule out choice A. Does a "mountain fill a hill"? No, so choice B is gone. Does "paint fill a watercolor"? Not in the same way that water fills an ocean, so we can rule out choice C. Does "ice fill glaciers"? Yes. Choice D is correct. (We would keep going and plug in choice E just to make sure that it wasn't a better fit, but choice D is correct).

The general steps to use this strategy are:

1. Make a sentence with question words
2. Plug answers into that sentence
3. Do NOT use the words could, maybe, can, sometimes- if you have to use those words the relationship is not strong enough

There are several relationships that show up frequently on the SSAT. If you become familiar with them, it makes it much easier to make up your own sentences quickly.

They are:

#1 Occupation- one word is the job of the other word
    ex: Architect is to building

#2 Part of- one word is a part of the other word
    ex: Kitchen is to house

#3 Type of- one word is a type of the other word, which is a broader category
    ex: Whale is to mammal

#4 Means without- one word means without the other word
    ex: Poor is to money

#5 Used for- one word is used to do the other word
    ex: Shovel is to dig

#6 Degree- the words have roughly the same meaning, only one is more extreme
    ex: Hungry is starving

#7 Characteristic of – one word is a characteristic of the other
    ex: Massive is to elephant

#8 Synonyms- the words have roughly the same meaning
    ex: Deceitful is to dishonest

9 Antonyms- the words are opposite in meaning
    ex: friendly is to rude

#10 Sequence- there is a distinct order that the words go in (months, time, etc.)
    ex: March is to July

#11 Found in- one word is found in the other
    ex: Shark is to ocean

Keep in mind that every single analogy on this test is not going to have one of these relationships. But the vast majority of the questions will.

For the following drill, provide the number of the relationship from above that the words use.

1. Instruct is to teacher – uses relationship # _____

2. Sonnet is to poem – uses relationship # _____

3. Seahorse is to ocean – uses relationship # _____

4. Flat is to plains – uses relationship # _____

5. Wrench is to tightening – uses relationship # _____

6. Processor is to computer – uses relationship # _____

7. Bleak is to hopeful – uses relationship # _____

8. Audacious is to bold – uses relationship # _____

9. Daybreak is to noon – uses relationship # _____

10. Camera is to picture – uses relationship # _____

(Answers to drills are found at the end of the verbal strategies section)

Strategy #2: If you don't know one of the question words, head to the answer choices

If you read through the question words and don't know what one (or both) of the question words mean, all is not lost. Sometimes there are answer choices with words that are not even related. Rule these out. Then plug the question words into the sentence you made from the remaining answer choices and see if it could work. Rule out any that don't. Guess from what you have left.

Here are the steps to this strategy:

1. Rule out answer choices that have unrelated words
2. Make a sentence with the remaining answer choices
3. Plug your question words into those sentences and see what could work
4. Remember to guess if you can rule out even one answer choice

Keep in mind that if you find yourself using "could" "maybe, "can", or "sometimes", it is not a strong relationship so you should rule it out. If you hear yourself using those words, you are talking yourself into a wrong answer choice!

- If you have to use could, maybe, can, or sometimes it is not a strong relationship and you should rule out that answer choice

Here is an example:

1. (Weird word) is to ship as
   (A) luck is to delay
   (B) fun is to laughter
   (C) helmet is to football
   (D) mansion is to house
   (E) first is to last

Since we don't know one question word, we go to the answers. If we try to make a sentence from choice A, we can see that luck and delay just don't have a strong relationship. You could say that if you are lucky, you might not have a delay. However, that would be talking yourself into a relationship isn't strong at all (if you have to use sometimes, might, may, could, it is not a good relationship). Choice A is out. For choice B, you could say that laughter is the result of fun. However, if we plug the question words back into that sentence, is there anything that ship is a result of? Not really, so we can rule out choice B. If we look at choice C, you could say that that a helmet is worn to play football. But if we plug our question words into that sentence, is there anything that worn to play ship? No. Choice C is out. On to choice D. A mansion is a type of house. Could something be a type of ship? Absolutely, so we keep choice D. Finally, choice E. First and last are opposites. But is there a word that means the opposite of ship? No, so choice E is out. We were able to narrow it down to one choice (choice D) without even knowing one of the question words.

For the following drill, you may not know one (or both!) of the question words. Rule out any answer choices that have words that are not related. From what is left, plug the question words into the sentence that you made from the answer choice. Rule out any answer choices that don't work. Remember, if you can rule out even one answer choice, then you should guess.

1. Contempt is to respect as
   (A) clever is to lazy
   (B) fast is to afraid
   (C) doubt is to delay
   (D) defined is to uncertainty
   (E) funny is to crowded

2. Nefarious is to villain
   (A) beneficent is to hero
   (B) crazy is to rock star
   (C) funny is to politician
   (D) loud is to nun
   (E) fast is to cast

3. Obliterate is to destroy
   (A) overlook is to film
   (B) build is to correct
   (C) horrify is to upset
   (D) ease is to worsen
   (E) ask is to function

4. Fortress is to stronghold
   (A) tiger is to lion
   (B) mansion is to shack
   (C) cuff is to shirt
   (D) criminal is to juvenile
   (E) car is to automobile

5. Cordial is to rude as
   (A) baffling is to strict
   (B) devoted is to mild
   (C) luxurious is to energetic
   (D) quaint is to sophisticated
   (E) cherished is to tough

(Answers to drills are found at the end of the verbal strategies section)

Answers to Synonyms and Analogies drills

Drill #1

1. C
2. A
3. B
4. D
5. E

Drill #2

1. A
2. E
3. B
4. C
5. D

Drill #3

1. D
2. D
3. A
4. B
5. C

Drill #4

1. B
2. C
3. E
4. A
5. D

Drill #5

1. C
2. B
3. E

Drill #6

1. #1
2. #3
3. #11
4. #7
5. #5
6. #2
7. #9
8. #8
9. #10
10. #5

Drill #7

1. D
2. A
3. C
4. E
5. D

Vocabulary Review

A key component of improving your verbal score is increasing your vocabulary. Following are ten lessons that will help you do just that.

If you have older sibling preparing for the Upper Level with our materials, you may notice that the vocabulary sections are the same in our Middle Level and Upper level books. This is because the words on the Middle and Upper Level synonym sections are the same levels. There are just a few more of the easier words on the Middle Level and a few more of the harder words on the Upper Level.

Each lesson has twenty new words for you to learn. There are good words, there are bad words, and there are even words with roots. Exciting, eh?

After you learn the words, complete the activities for each lesson. The best way to learn new words is to think of them in categories and to evaluate how the words relate to one another. The activities will help you do this.

The activities also give you practice with synonyms and analogies. You will be working on strategy while you are learning new words- think of it as a two for one!

If there are words that you have trouble remembering as you work through the lessons, go ahead and make flashcards for them. Continue to review these flashcards until the words stick. There may also be words that you run across in the analogies or synonyms practice that you do not know the meaning of. Make flashcards for these words as well.

After each lesson are the answers. Be sure to check your work.

Now, on to the lessons!

Lesson One

Words to Learn

Below are the twenty words used in Lesson One; refer back to this list as needed as you move through the lesson.

Marina: dock
Trivial: unimportant
Terrain: ground
Apathetic: disinterested
Calamity: disaster

Devastate: destroy
Sentient: aware
Mariner: sailor
Grapple: struggle
Inter: bury

Cognizant: informed
Ameliorate: improve
Prosperity: good fortune
Aloof: withdrawn
Perceptive: sensitive

Adversity: misfortune
Subterranean: underground
Crucial: important
Submarine: underwater
Oblivious: unaware

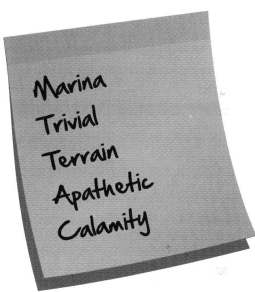

Word List Practice

Use the words from the list above to complete the following activities.

List three words that describe a person who doesn't know or doesn't care.
1.
2.
3.

List three words that could describe a person who knows what is going on.
1.
2.
3.

List three words that have a decidedly negative meaning.
1.
2.
3.

Analogies Practice

One of the common relationships used in the analogy part of the test is the antonym relationship. In this relationship, words are used that are opposite in meaning.

To complete the questions below, use the following word bank:
Sentient
Adversity
Trivial
Oblivious

Use the antonym relationship and the list of words above to complete the following questions.

1. Happy is to sad as prosperity is to _____.

2. Fearless is to scared as cognizant is to _____.

3. Good is to bad as crucial is to _____.

4. Joy is to pain as aloof is to _____.

Roots practice

Below are three words. Write the definition for the words on the line provided. Based on their meanings, define the common root.

Marina _____

Mariner _____

Submarine _____

1. The root "mar" means:

   Inter _____

   Subterranean _____

   Terrain _____

2. The root "terr/ter" means:

3. If "aqu/a" is the root meaning water, what do you think the word "aquamarine" means?

4. Based on the roots terr/ter and aqu/a, what do you think the word "terraqueous" means?

5. Based on the words submarine and subterranean, can you figure out the meaning of the root "sub?"

Synonyms Practice

1. CALAMITY
   (A) laughter
   (B) disaster
   (C) heaven
   (D) species
   (E) morale

2. DEVASTATE
   (A) help
   (B) forgive
   (C) glow
   (D) destroy
   (E) break

3. AMELIORATE
   (A) improve
   (B) cook
   (C) construct
   (D) relax
   (E) defy

4. GRAPPLE
   (A) release
   (B) remember
   (C) struggle
   (D) blend
   (E) incorporate

5. PERCEPTIVE
   (A) ignorant
   (B) convivial
   (C) incompatible
   (D) dense
   (E) sensitive

6. APATHETIC
   (A) enthusiastic
   (B) overjoyed
   (C) hyper
   (D) disinterested
   (E) tired

7. CRUCIAL
   (A) loud
   (B) miniature
   (C) important
   (D) late
   (E) crunchy

Answers to Lesson One

Word List Practice

1. apathetic
2. aloof
3. oblivious

1. sentient
2. cognizant
3. perceptive

1. calamity
2. devastate
3. adversity

Analogy Practice

1. adversity
2. oblivious
3. trivial
4. sentient

Roots Practice

1. sea
2. earth
3. color of sea water
4. formed of land and water
5. under/beneath

Synonyms Practice

1. B
2. D
3. A
4. C
5. E
6. D
7. C

Lesson Two

Words to Learn

Below are the twenty words used in Lesson Two; refer back to this list as needed as you move through the lesson.

Enunciate: pronounce
Procrastinate: delay
Inscribe: write
Cleave: split
Magnitude: importance

Abashed: embarrassed
Indescribable: beyond words
Denigrate: criticize
Hew: cut
Figurative: symbolic

Grotesque: ugly
Proscribe: forbid
Corpulent: fat
Eminence: superiority
Incorporate: include

Metaphorical: figurative (not literal)
Repugnant: loathsome (nasty)
Exhilarated: elated (thrilled)
Manifest: demonstrate
Corporeal: bodily

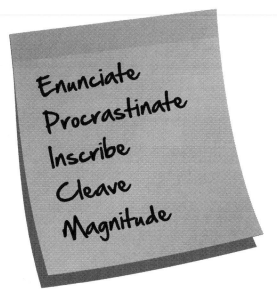

Word List Practice

Use the words from the list above to complete the following activities.

List three words that describe something you could do to someone.
1.

2.

3.

4. If you called someone "corpulent," they might think that you are _____.

5. If you realized at school that your pants were cleaved in two, you would probably feel _____.

Analogy Practice

One of the common relationships used in the analogy part of the test is the synonym relationship. This relationship uses words that have the same meaning.

To complete the questions below, use the following word bank:

Metaphorical
Procrastinate
Hew
Repugnant

Use the synonym relationship and the list of words above to complete the following questions.

1. Mock is to tease as cleave is to _____.

2. Clear is to translucent as figurative is to _____.

3. Jump is to hop as delay is to _____.

4. Calm is to placid as grotesque is to _____.

Roots Practice

Below are three words. Write the definition for the words on the line provided. Based on their meanings, define the common root.

Inscribe _____

Proscribe _____

Indescribable _____

1. The root "scribe" means:

Corpulent _____

Incorporate _____

Corporeal _____

2. The root "corp" means:

3. Based on the meaning of "corp," what popular term for business also means "body of men?" (This is not a word from our lesson, but rather one you might know from another place) _____

4. A doctor has to _____ many drugs before you can take them (this word is similar to one of the words in this lesson, but it is NOT that word!).

5. Based on one of the roots above, can you think of a term meaning "one who writes?"

_____

Synonyms Practice

Since you practiced with synonyms in the analogy section, use the crossword below to spend more time with the words from this lesson.

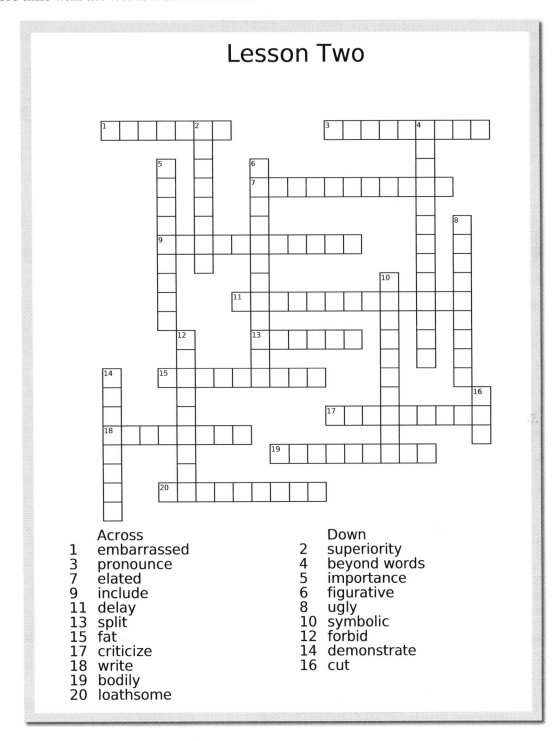

Lesson Two

Across
1. embarrassed
3. pronounce
7. elated
9. include
11. delay
13. split
15. fat
17. criticize
18. write
19. bodily
20. loathsome

Down
2. superiority
4. beyond words
5. importance
6. figurative
8. ugly
10. symbolic
12. forbid
14. demonstrate
16. cut

Answers to Lesson Two

Word List Practice

1. proscribe
2. denigrate
3. incorporate
4. repugnant
5. abashed

Analogy Practice

1. hew
2. metaphorical
3. procrastinate
4. repugnant

Roots Practice

1. to write
2. body
3. corporation
4. prescribe
5. scribe

Synonym Crossword

1. abashed
2. eminence
3. enunciate
4. indescribable
5. magnitude
6. metaphorical
7. exhilarated
8. grotesque
9. incorporate
10. figurative
11. procrastinate
12. proscribe
13. cleave
14. manifest
15. corpulent
16. hew
17. denigrate
18. inscribe
19. corporeal
20. repugnant

Lesson Three

Words to Learn

Below are the twenty words used in Lesson Three; refer back to this list as needed as you move through the lesson.

Animate: enliven (bring to life)
Boisterous: noisy
Paraphrase: summarize
Irate: angry
Rejuvenate: refresh

Surfeit: excess
Circumvent: go around
Magnanimous: generous
Vitality: energy
Fractious: bad-tempered

Ravenous: starving
Equanimity: composure (calmness)
Intimidate: frighten
Miscreant: villain
Satiated: satisfied

Vivacious: lively
Craving: hunger or desire
Incensed: enraged
Convivial: friendly
Culprit: wrongdoer

Animate
Boisterous
Paraphrase
Irate
Rejuvenate

Word List Practice

Use the words from the list above to complete the following activities.

1. Would you rather spend time with someone who is fractious or convivial? _____

2. If you were rejuvenated, you would have more _____.

List three words that can be related to eating and/or being hungry:
   1.

   2.

   3.

Analogy Practice

One of the common relationships used in the analogy part of the test is the degree relationship. In this relationship, the words have roughly the same meaning, only one word is more extreme than the other word.

To complete the questions below, use the following word bank:

Miscreant
Incensed
Surfeit
Ravenous

Use the degree relationship and the list of words above to complete the following questions.

1. Happy is to exhilarated as craving is to _____.

2. Sadness is to depression as culprit is to _____.

3. Cold is to icy as irate is to _____.

4. Lack is to dearth as plenty is to _____.

Roots practice

Below are three words. Write the definition for the words on the line provided. Based on their meanings, define the common root.

Animate _____

Equanimity _____

Magnanimous _____

1. The root "anim" means:

    Vivacious _____

    Vitality _____

    Convivial _____

2. The root "vi/viv" means:

3. Based on the meaning of the root "anim," why do you think cartoons are called "animation?"

4. The root "magna" means large. What is an alternate definition of "magnanimous," using its two roots?

5. If "oviparous" means producing young in eggs, based on one of the roots above, what do you think the word "viviparous" means?

Synonyms Practice

1. BOISTEROUS
   (A) happy
   (B) uncoordinated
   (C) noisy
   (D) silly
   (E) sad

2. PARAPHRASE
   (A) forget
   (B) give away
   (C) release
   (D) summarize
   (E) take

3. CIRCUMVENT
   (A) frighten
   (B) go around
   (C) jump
   (D) drive
   (E) cross

4. FRACTIOUS
   (A) bad-tempered
   (B) overjoyed
   (C) despondent
   (D) crucial
   (E) hardworking

5. INTIMIDATE
   (A) alleviate
   (B) resist
   (C) boil
   (D) conspire
   (E) frighten

6. REJUVENATE
   (A) drain
   (B) refresh
   (C) assist
   (D) wash
   (E) create

Answers to Lesson Three

Word List Practice

1. convivial
2. vitality

1. craving
2. ravenous
3. satiated

Analogy Practice

1. ravenous
2. miscreant
3. incensed
4. surfeit

Roots Practice

1. life, spirit
2. life
3. cartoons bring drawings or still images to life
4. large spirit
5. producing live young

Synonyms Practice

1. C
2. D
3. B
4. A
5. E
6. B

Lesson Four

Words to Learn

Below are the twenty words used in Lesson Four; refer back to this list as needed as you move through the lesson.

Pandemonium: uproar
Hierarchy: ranked system
Subsist: exist (barely get by)
Eulogy: speech in praise
Unwittingly: unknowingly

Paraphernalia: belongings
Desist: cease (stop)
Cadaverous: ghastly (ghost-like)
Imminent: impending (about to happen)
Agitator: troublemaker

Wrangle: dispute
Deciduous: falling off
Prevalent: widespread
Stagnant: sluggish (not moving)
Decadence: decline

Epiphany: insight
Accolades: praise
Serf: slave
Pilgrimage: journey
Reimburse: pay back

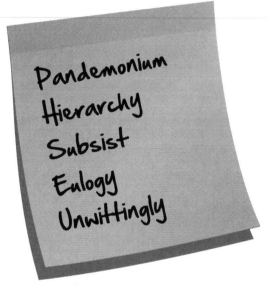

Pandemonium
Hierarchy
Subsist
Eulogy
Unwittingly

Word List Practice

Use the words from the list above to complete the following activities.

1. Your parents probably give you this for bringing home good grades.

2. Trees with leaves that turn colors each fall are called deciduous. Why?

3. A speech written for a funeral is called a _____.

4. Though often used to describe rich desserts and other food or pleasure, this word actually means something negative:

Analogy Practice

One of the common relationships used in the analogy part of the SSAT is the "found in" relationship. In this relationship, one word is found in the other, such as "fish is to sea".

To complete the questions below, use the following word bank:

Serf
Paraphernalia
Eulogy
Pandemonium

Use the "found in" relationship and the list of words above to complete the following questions.

1. Animal is to zoo as agitator is to _____.

2. Beans are to burrito as accolades are to _____.

3. Jail is to prisoner as farm is to _____.

4. Suitcase is to clothes as a bag is to _____.

Roots Practice

Below are three words. Write the definition for the words on the line provided. Based on their meanings, define the common root.

Subsist _____

Desist _____

Stagnant _____

1. The root "sist/sta" means:

Cadaverous _____

Decadence _____

Deciduous _____

2. The root "cad/cid" means:

3. Based on desist, decadence, and deciduous, what do you think the root "de" means?

4. Based on the meaning of "cadaverous," what does the word "cadaver" mean?

5. If the root "cad" means "to fall," what did a "cadaver" fall from?

6. What makes water "stagnant?"

Synonym Practice

To spend some more time with the words from this lesson, complete the crossword below.

Lesson Four

Across

3. pay back
4. sluggish
5. ranked system
7. slave
8. cease
9. decline
11. belongings
14. journey
15. falling off
17. unknowingly
19. exist
20. troublemaker

Down

1. widespread
2. dispute
6. ghastly
10. uproar
12. praise
13. insight
16. speech in praise
18. impending

Answers to Lesson Four

Word List Practice

1. accolades
2. because the leaves fall off
3. eulogy
4. decadence

Analogy Practice

1. pandemonium
2. eulogy
3. serf
4. paraphernalia

Roots Practice

1. stand
2. to fall
3. opposite or away from
4. corpse
5. life
6. If water is standing or not moving, it becomes stagnant.

Synonym Crossword

1. Prevalent
2. Wrangle
3. Reimburse
4. Stagnant
5. Hierarchy
6. Cadaverous
7. Serf
8. Desist
9. Decadence
10. Pandemonium
11. Paraphernalia
12. Accolades
13. Epiphany
14. Pilgrimage
15. Deciduous
16. Eulogy
17. Unwittingly
18. Imminent
19. Subsist
20. Agitator

Lesson Five

Words to Learn

Below are the twenty words used in Lesson Five; refer back to this list as needed as you move through the lesson.

Pragmatic: sensible
Mercurial: temperamental (moody)
Morose: depressed
Frustrate: disappoint
Serene: calm

Carnivorous: meat-eating
Ostentatious: flashy
Insolent: disrespectful
Omniscient: all-knowing
Effervescent: bubbly

Stupendous: wonderful
Incarnation: embodiment (a spirit being born into a body)
Omnivorous: eats everything
Impetuous: impulsive
Mediocre: unexceptional

Grovel: beg
Reincarnation: rebirth
Omnipotent: all-powerful
Interminable: boring
Fraudulent: deceptive

Word List Practice

Use the words from the list above to complete the following activities.

1. Would you rather have a mediocre meal or a stupendous meal?

2. It would be _____ for the bank to tell you that your account had $100 in it, when you had actually deposited $500.

3. _____ people think through decisions. Those who are _____ often do not.

Analogy Practice

One of the common relationships used in the analogy part of the test is the "characteristic of" relationship. In this relationship, one word is a characteristic of the other word, such as "tiny is to ant".

To complete the questions below, use the following word bank:

Serene
Ostentatious
Interminable
Effervescent
Mercurial

Use the "characteristic of" relationship and the list of words above to complete the following questions.

1. Elephant is to massive as long lines is to _____.

2. Ice is to freezing as Las Vegas is to _____.

3. Silk is to smooth as pacifist is to _____.

4. Sugar is to sweet as carbonated beverages is to _____.

5. Hero is to brave as toddler is to _____.

Roots practice

Below are three words. Write the definition for the words on the line provided. Based on their meanings, define the common root.

Carnivorous _____

Incarnation _____

Reincarnation _____

1. The root "carn" means:

Omniscient _____

Omnipotent _____

Omnivorous _____

2. The root "omni" means:

3. If an "herbivore" eats plants, what does a "carnivore" eat?

4. What, then, does an "omnivore" eat?

5. Based on the meaning of the root, for whom does an "omnibus" provide transportation?

6. Based on the meanings of "incarnation" and "reincarnation," what do you think the root "re" means?

Synonym Practice

1. INSOLENT
   - (A) happy
   - (B) frightened
   - (C) disrespectful
   - (D) furious
   - (E) timid

2. IMPETUOUS
   - (A) disillusioned
   - (B) impulsive
   - (C) curious
   - (D) smooth
   - (E) beautiful

3. MOROSE
   - (A) gleeful
   - (B) conciliatory
   - (C) jaded
   - (D) depressed
   - (E) sleepy

4. GROVEL
   - (A) beg
   - (B) answer
   - (C) touch
   - (D) flee
   - (E) forgive

5. FRUSTRATE
   - (A) assist
   - (B) locate
   - (C) endure
   - (D) master
   - (E) disappoint

6. MEDIOCRE
   - (A) grand
   - (B) unexceptional
   - (C) easy
   - (D) constricted
   - (E) forgotten

Answers to Lesson Five

Word List Practice

1. stupendous
2. fraudulent
3. pragmatic; impetuous

Analogy Practice

1. interminable
2. ostentatious
3. serene
4. effervescent
5. mercurial

Roots Practice

1. flesh
2. all, every
3. flesh (meat)
4. everything
5. everyone (many people)
6. back, again

Synonyms Practice

1. C
2. B
3. D
4. A
5. E
6. B

Lesson Six

Words to Learn

Below are the twenty words used in Lesson Six; refer back to this list as needed as you move through the lesson.

Disdain: scorn
Prognosis: forecast
Bias: prejudice
Lenient: permissive
Jaded: indifferent (not easily impressed)

Philanthropy: humanitarianism (giving to people in need)
Limpid: clear
Confound: confuse
Diagnose: identify
Arrogant: proud

Arduous: difficult
Philosophy: beliefs
Bellicose: belligerent (looking for a fight)
Compassion: pity
Consensus: agreement

Bibliophile: booklover
Humility: modesty
Gnostic: wise
Distort: warp
Haphazard: disorganized

Disdain
Prognosis
Bias
Lenient
Jaded

Word List Practice

Use the words from the list above to complete the following activities.

1. What word found in the word list is an antonym for humble (the adjective form of the word humility)?

2. Most people want their parents to be more _____ when it comes to curfews and house rules.

3. It can be hard for _____ people to reach a consensus with people that they disagree with.

4. It is easy to become confounded when instructions are _____.

5. Studying for exams like the SSAT is an _____ process.

Analogy Practice

One of the common relationships used in the analogy part of the test is the "means without" relationship. In this relationship, one word means without the other word, such as "freedom is to prison".

To complete the questions below, use the following word bank:

Disdain
Jaded
Arduousness
Bellicose
Arrogance

Use the "means without" relationship and the list of words above to complete the following questions.

1. Hearing is to deaf as naivety is to_____ .

2. Food is to starving as peace is to _____.

3. Poor is to money as compassion is to _____.

4. Naked is to clothing as humble is to _____ .

5. Blind is to sight as ease is to _____.

Roots Practice

Below are three words. Write the definition for the words on the line provided. Based on their meanings, define the common root.

Philanthropy _____

Philosophy _____

Bibliophile _____

1. The root "phil" means:

Prognosis _____

Diagnose _____

Gnostic _____

2. The root "gnos" means:

3. If the root "soph" means "wise," what is a meaning of "philosophy" derived directly from its two roots?

4. Based on the meaning of "prognosis," what does someone who "prognosticates" do?

5. If the root "anthro" means "man," what is a meaning of "philanthropy" derived directly from its two roots?

Synonym Practice

Use the crossword below to spend more time with the words in this lesson.

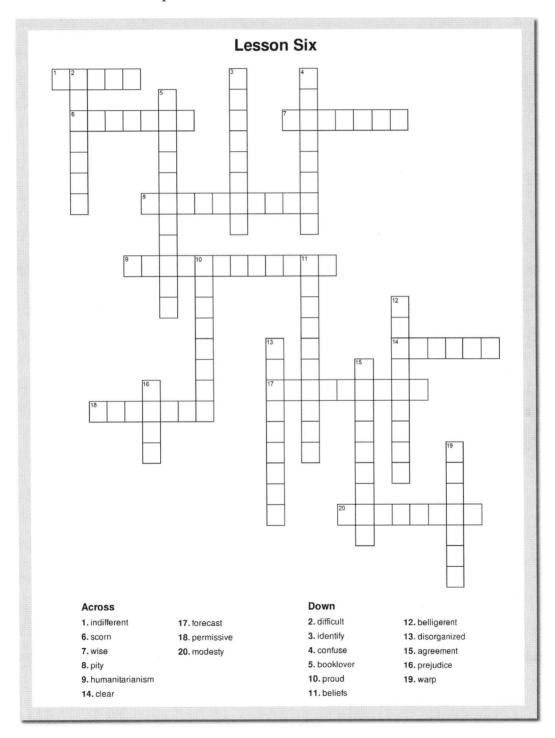

Lesson Six

Across

1. indifferent
6. scorn
7. wise
8. pity
9. humanitarianism
14. clear
17. forecast
18. permissive
20. modesty

Down

2. difficult
3. identify
4. confuse
5. booklover
10. proud
11. beliefs
12. belligerent
13. disorganized
15. agreement
16. prejudice
19. warp

Answers to Lesson Six

Word List

1. arrogant
2. lenient
3. bellicose
4. haphazard
5. arduous

Analogy

1. jaded
2. bellicose
3. disdain
4. arrogance
5. arduousness

Roots

1. love of
2. know
3. love of wisdom
4. they foretell or prophesy
5. love of man(kind)

Synonym Crossword

1. Jaded
2. Arduous
3. Diagnose
4. Confound
5. Bibliophile
6. Disdain
7. Gnostic
8. Compassion
9. Philanthropy
10. Arrogant
11. Philosophy
12. Bellicose
13. Haphazard
14. Limpid
15. Consensus
16. Bias
17. Prognosis
18. Lenient
19. Distort
20. Humility

Lesson Seven

Words to Learn

Below are the twenty words used in Lesson Seven; refer back to this list as needed as you move through the lesson.

Mediator: negotiator
Allege: claim
Deficient: lacking
Eloquent: expressive
Exasperate: irritate

Facile: easy
Artifice: hoax (deceptive trick)
Frivolous: light-minded
Ecstasy: rapture (extreme happiness)
Proletariat: workers

Mortician: undertaker (funeral home worker)
Facilitate: help
Confection: candy
Notary: public official (who verifies signatures)
Dynamic: energetic

Facsimile: copy
Psychiatrist: therapist
Absolution: forgiveness
Cursory: brief
Lobbyist: advocate

Word List Practice

Use the words from the list above to complete the following activities.

List the five words that describe a job or occupation:

1.
2.
3.
4.
5.

6. It's best not to take a _____ look at these words, but rather to spend some time with them.

Analogy Practice

One of the common relationships used in the analogy section of the test is the "occupation" relationship. In this relationship, one word means the job of the other word, such as "architect is to building".

To complete the questions below, use the following word bank:

Notary
Mediator
Lobbyist
Proletariat
Psychiatrist

Use the "occupation" relationship and the list of words above to complete the following questions.

1. Legality is to lawyer as mental health is to _____.

2. Build is to contractor as advocate is to _____.

3. Article is to journalist as document is _____.

4. Ceramics is to potter as agreement is to _____.

5. Surgery is to doctor as manual labor is to _____.

Roots Practice

Below are three words. Write the definition for the words on the line provided. Based on their meanings, define the common root.

Facsimile _____

Facile _____

Facilitate _____

1. The root "fac" means:

   Artifice _____

   Deficient _____

   Confection _____

2. The root "fic/fect" means:

3. Give an alternate definition for "facilitate," using the root and the definition of "facile": to _____ .

4. Based on one of the roots above, what do you think happens in a factory?

5. If the root "magni" means great, using one of the roots above, what could the definition of "magnificent" be?

6. If something is "artificial," do you think it is created by man or does it occur in nature?

Synonym Practice

1. FRIVOLOUS
   (A) serious
   (B) active
   (C) light-minded
   (D) bashful
   (E) ornery

2. ELOQUENT
   (A) expressive
   (B) certain
   (C) terrified
   (D) rapacious
   (E) chatty

3. ALLEGE
   (A) lie
   (B) frighten
   (C) leap
   (D) sigh
   (E) claim

4. DYNAMIC
   (A) goofy
   (B) energetic
   (C) distinguished
   (D) hopeful
   (E) happy

5. ECSTASY
   (A) rage
   (B) hope
   (C) truth
   (D) rapture
   (E) fear

6. CURSORY
   (A) brief
   (B) easy
   (C) convoluted
   (D) shy
   (E) complicated

7. EXASPERATE
   (A) subdue
   (B) irritate
   (C) trace
   (D) behave
   (E) despise

8. ABSOLUTION
   (A) dinner
   (B) honesty
   (C) scent
   (D) pile
   (E) forgiveness

Answers to Lesson Seven

Word List Practice

1. psychiatrist
2. mortician
3. mediator
4. lobbyist
5. notary
6. cursory

Roots practice

1. to make, to do
2. to make
3. make easy
4. things are *made*
5. made greatly
6. made by man

Analogy Practice

1. psychiatrist
2. lobbyist
3. notary
4. mediator
5. proletariat

Synonym Practice

1. C
2. A
3. E
4. B
5. D
6. A
7. B
8. E

Lesson Eight

Words to Learn

Below are the twenty words used in Lesson Eight; refer back to this list as needed as you move through the lesson.

Nostalgia: longing
Precocious: advanced
Elegy: funeral song
Recuperate: recover
Enhance: increase

Posterity: descendants
Excavate: dig
Precaution: carefulness
Futile: useless
Undaunted: unafraid

Litigation: legal proceeding
Prelude: introduction
Instigate: provoke (start a fight)
Curriculum: studies
Fluctuate: waver

Demoralize: depress
Posthumous: after death
Deteriorate: worsen
Posterior: rear
Curvature: arc

Nostalgia
Precocious
Elegy
Recuperate
Enhance

Word List Practice

Use the words from the list above to complete the following activities.

1. If a book was published posthumously, would the author be able to read the finished edition? Why or why not?

2. Would a superhero more likely be described as demoralized or undaunted?

3. If something doesn't get better, it either stays the same or it _____.

4. It takes a long time to _____ after an illness like whooping cough.

Analogy Practice

One of the common relationships used in the analogy part of the SSAT is the "used for" relationship. In this relationship, one word is used for the other word, such as "voice is to sing".

To complete the questions below, use the following word bank:

Excavate
Litigation
Elegy
Curriculum

Use the "used for" relationship and the list of words above to complete the following questions.

1. Car is to transportation as jazz procession is to _____.

2. Recipe is to meal as lesson plans are to _____.

3. Pen is to writing as legal maneuver is to _____.

4. Broom is to sweep as shovel is to _____.

Root practice

Below are three words. Write the definition for the words on the line provided. Based on their meanings, define the common root.

Posterior _____

Posterity _____

Posthumous _____

1. The root "post" means:

Prelude _____

Precocious _____

Precaution _____

2. The root "pre" means:

3. How does the meaning of the root "pre" factor into the meaning of "precocious?" If someone is "precocious," they are "advanced before" what?

4. There is another word meaning "after death" that uses the root words "post" and "mort." Can you guess what it is?

5. If the root word "inter" means "between," and a prelude is an introduction, when do you think an "interlude" happens?

6. If "posterior" means at the end (or rear), what very similar word means "at the beginning?" (Hint: ante means before)

Synonym Practice

To spend more time with the words in this lesson, complete the crossword puzzle below.

Lesson Eight

Across

2. longing
3. depress
5. worsen
8. after death
10. carefulness
11. introduction
13. recover
15. provoke
17. unafraid
18. increase
19. useless

Down

1. legal proceeding
4. advanced
6. waver
7. descendants
9. studies
12. rear
14. dig
16. arc
20. funeral song

Answers to Lesson Eight

Word List Practice

1. no, because the author would be dead
2. undaunted
3. deteriorates
4. recuperate

Analogy Practice

1. elegy
2. curriculum
3. litigation
4. excavate

Roots Practice

1. after, behind
2. before
3. what is normal for his or her age
4. postmortem
5. in the middle
6. anterior

Synonym Crossword

1. Litigation
2. Nostalgia
3. Demoralize
4. Precocious
5. Deteriorate
6. Fluctuate
7. Posterity
8. Posthumous
9. Curriculum
10. Precaution
11. Prelude
12. Posterior
13. Recuperate
14. Excavate
15. Instigate
16. Curvature
17. Undaunted
18. Enhance
19. Futile
20. Elegy

Lesson Nine

Words to Learn

Below are the twenty words used in Lesson Nine; refer back to this list as needed as you move through the lesson.

Potent: powerful
Collaborate: cooperate
Retribution: punishment
Burnish: polish
Convergence: union

Stalwart: robust (strong and dependable)
Coincide: correspond (happen at the same time)
Gusto: enjoyment
Spontaneous: impulsive
Zealous: fervent (passionate)

Deflect: divert (turn away)
Fortuitous: lucky
Succinct: brief
Genuflect: kneel
Deliberate: intentional

Premeditated: planned
Voluble: talkative
Inflection: tone (of voice)
Hybrid: mixed
Resolute: determined

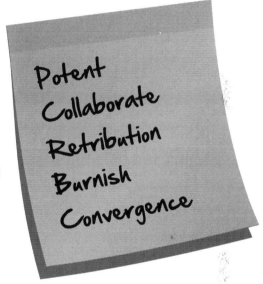

Potent
Collaborate
Retribution
Burnish
Convergence

Word List Practice

Use the words from the list above to complete the following activities.

When we are electing the next president, we hope that he or she is what three things from the list above?

1.
2.
3.

4. If we have to watch her give a speech, however, we hope that she is not _____.

5. What is "mixed" about a hybrid car?

6. Is winning the lottery "fortuitous" or "deliberate?"

Analogy Practice

This lesson will give you more practice with the antonym relationship. Remember, antonyms are words with opposite meanings.

To complete the questions below, use the following word bank:

Potent
Deliberate
Spontaneous
Voluble

Use the antonym relationship and the list of words above to complete the following questions.

1. Up is to down as fortuitous is to _____.

2. In is to out as succinct is to _____.

3. Hard is to soft as powerless is to _____.

4. Wet is to dry as premeditated is to _____.

Root Practice

Below are three words. Write the definition for the words on the line provided. Based on their meanings, define the common root.

Deflect _____

Genuflect _____

Inflection _____

1. The root "flect" means:

    Convergence _____

    Coincide _____

    Collaborate _____

2. The root "co/con" means:

3. What "bends" when it comes to inflection?

4. What "bends" when someone genuflects?

5. If an "incident" is an event or occurrence, what happens in a "coincidence?"

6. Using the meaning of the root "di" (apart) and the word convergence, what is a word meaning "to go in different directions from a common point?"

Synonym Practice

1. BURNISH
   (A) reduce
   (B) roll
   (C) light
   (D) polish
   (E) strike

2. ZEALOUS
   (A) hyper
   (B) peaceful
   (C) ragged
   (D) slow
   (E) fervent

3. STALWART
   (A) weak
   (B) shy
   (C) unavailable
   (D) robust
   (E) tired

4. GUSTO
   (A) hope
   (B) fear
   (C) enjoyment
   (D) certitude
   (E) flight

5. RETRIBUTION
   (A) punishment
   (B) glee
   (C) enjoyment
   (D) happiness
   (E) planning

6. HYBRID
   (A) sore
   (B) mixed
   (C) clean
   (D) spinning
   (E) clear

Answers to Lesson Nine

Word List Practice

1. potent
2. stalwart
3. resolute
4. voluble
5. power sources for the engine: gasoline and electric
6. fortuitous

Analogy

1. deliberate
2. voluble
3. potent
4. spontaneous

Roots

1. to bend
2. with, together
3. a voice, or the tone of a voice
4. knees
5. two events come together
6. diverge

Synonyms

1. D
2. E
3. D
4. C
5. A
6. B

Lesson Ten

Words to Learn

Below are the twenty words used in Lesson Ten; refer back to this list as needed as you move through the lesson.

Sustenance: nourishment
Lackluster: dull
Trajectory: path
Insurgent: rebel
Genesis: origin

Antagonistic: hostile
Illustrious: celebrated
Unkempt: messy
Trite: overused
Insurrection: revolt

Contemplate: ponder (think about)
Vogue: popularity
Lustrous: shining
Resurrect: bring back
Excruciating: agonizing

Subsistence: survival
Provenance: birthplace
Duplicity: deceptiveness
Ruminate: reflect
Averse: opposing

Sustenance
Lackluster
Trajectory
Insurgent
Genesis

Word List Practice

Use the words from the list above to complete the following activities.

List three words from above that you would like to have associated with you:

1.

2.

3.

List three words from above that you would NOT like to have associated with you:

4.

5.

6.

7. If a definition of "subsist" is "keep going," do you think subsistence living includes luxuries? Why or why not?

Analogy Practice

This lesson will give you more practice with the synonym relationship. Remember, synonyms are words with the same meaning.

To complete the questions below, use the following word bank:

Genesis
Antagonistic
Ruminate
Unkempt

Use the synonym relationship and the list of words above to complete the following questions.

1. Plush is to comfortable as averse is to _____.

2. Seek is to search as contemplate is to _____.

3. Illustrious is to celebrated as messy is to _____.

4. Provenance is to birthplace as creation is to _____.

Root Practice

Below are three words. Write the definition for the words on the line provided. Based on their meanings, define the common root.

Insurgent _____

Resurrect _____

Insurrection _____

1. The root "surg/surr" means:

Lackluster _____

Lustrous _____

Illustrious _____

2. The root "lust" means:

3. Do you think supermodels prefer their hair to be "lackluster" or "lustrous?"

4. Based on the meaning of "resurrect," what do you think "resurrection" means?

5. Based on the meaning of one of the roots above, what do you think it means when the tide "surges?"

Synonym Practice

Use the crossword puzzle below to spend more time with the words in this lesson.

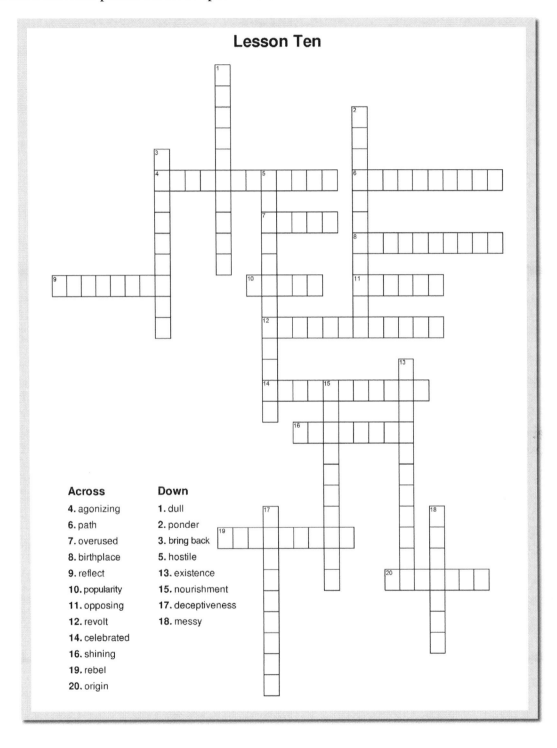

Lesson Ten

Across

4. agonizing
6. path
7. overused
8. birthplace
9. reflect
10. popularity
11. opposing
12. revolt
14. celebrated
16. shining
19. rebel
20. origin

Down

1. dull
2. ponder
3. bring back
5. hostile
13. existence
15. nourishment
17. deceptiveness
18. messy

Answers to Lesson Ten

Word List Practice

1. vogue
2. illustrious
3. lustrous
4. lackluster
5. unkempt
6. antagonistic
7. No – because you are living with just enough to keep going or just enough for existence.

Analogy Practice

1. antagonistic
2. ruminate
3. unkempt
4. genesis

Root Practice

1. rise
2. shine
3. lustrous
4. the act of being brought back to life
5. the tides rise

Synonym Crossword

1. Lackluster
2. Contemplate
3. Resurrect
4. Excruciating
5. Antagonistic
6. Trajectory
7. Trite
8. Provenance
9. Ruminate
10. Vogue
11. Averse
12. Insurrection
13. Subsistence
14. Illustrious
15. Sustenance
16. Lustrous
17. Duplicity
18. Unkempt
19. Insurgent
20. Genesis

SSAT Reading Section

In the SSAT reading section, you are given passages and then asked questions about these passages. In general, there tends to be about seven passages in this section, but there can be slightly more or slightly less. There also tends to be four to six questions per passage, but again this is only a general guideline. For the entire section, there will be a total of forty questions. You will have forty minutes to complete the section. There will be only one reading section on your test.

- About 7 passages (can be more or less, though)
- Roughly 4-6 questions for each passage
- 40 total questions
- 40 minutes to complete section
- Only one reading section

You may be thinking, I know how to read, I am good on this section. However, most people applying to independent school know how to read. In order to get the median 50th percentile score on the Middle Level on the reading section, you need to get a little more than half the questions correct (and not answer the others). This means that half the students taking this test are getting less than that. In fact, I have had 5th grade students only answer ¾ of the questions correctly and still score in the 99th percentile (which is the highest possible score).

- To get the median score for the Middle Level, you need to get a little more than half of the questions correct (and not answer the others)

The issue is that not every student can get a perfect score on the reading section, so the test writers have to create a test where some students who know how to read are going to miss several questions.

So how do the test writers get you to answer so many questions incorrectly? First of all, the questions can be very detail oriented. Think of this not as a reading test, but as looking for a needle in a haystack- with very little time to find it. Secondly, they include answer choices that take the words from the passage and switch them around so that all the same words are there… but the combination suddenly means something else. Lastly, they use your own brain against you! How do they do this?? As we read, we automatically fill in details to create a bigger picture. On this test, however, these details are often the wrong answer choices.

- Very detail-oriented questions
- Test writers rearrange words from passage to mean something else in an answer choice
- We fill in details as we read, but they aren't always correct

By making a plan and sticking to it, however, you can overcome these obstacles and beat the average score- by a lot!

In this section, first we will cover the general plan of attack and then we will get into the details that make the difference.

Reading Section Plan of Attack

Students can significantly improve their reading scores by following an easy plan:

Step 1: Plan your time
> Know how many passages there are, how many passages you need to answer before you are halfway through, and at what time you should be halfway through the passages.

Step 2: Prioritize passages
> Play to your strengths. Don't just answer the passages in the order that they appear.

Step 3: Go to the questions first
> Mark questions as either specific or general. You want to know what to look for as you read.

Step 4: Read the passage
> If you run across the answer to a specific question as you are reading, go ahead and answer that. But do not worry if you miss an answer.

Step 5: Answer specific questions
> If there are any specific questions that you did not answer yet, go back and find the answers.

Step 6: Answer general questions
> Answer any questions that ask about the passage as a whole.

Step 7: Repeat steps 3-6 with next passage
> You've got it under control. Just keep cranking through the section until you are done.

Keep in mind that this section is not a test of how well you read. It is a test of how well you test. You need to manage your time and think about the process rather than the actual reading.

Step #1- Plan your time

Before you do anything, take thirty seconds to plan out how much time you have to complete half of the passages. To do this, count up the total number of passages and then divide this number by 2.

- If you have six passages, you should be done with about three passages when you are 20 minutes into the reading section
- If you have 7 passages, you should have completed about three and a half of the passages when you are 20 minutes into the reading section
- If you have eight passages, you should have completed about four passages when you are 20 minutes into the reading section.

Now look at the starting time and make a quick chart of starting, time, halfway point, and ending time. For example, let's say that you have a section with 7 passages and you start at 9:23, then your chart should look like this:

Start- 9:23
Halfway point-9:43
End- 10:03

Note that the number of passages is not even divisible by two. This means that we have to guess-timate whether we are done with "half" a passage. Basically, in this example if you have only completed three passages at the halfway point, you need to speed it up. If you have started and made progress on the fourth passage at the halfway point, then you are right on track. If you have completed four passages at this halfway point, that is good because you have saved your hardest passages for last. If you have done five passages at the halfway point, however, you are rushing.

Drill #1

Let's say you start a reading section at 9:32 and there are 8 passages. Fill in the chart below (be sure to fill in both time and number of passages completed for the halfway point):

Start-

Halfway point-

Finish-

Now let's say you start a reading section at 8:56 and there are 7 passages. Make your own chart below:

(You can check your answers at the end of this reading section)

These times will give you rough milestones as you move through the test. Not every section will take you exactly the same amount of time, so don't stress if a long passage with six questions takes you a little longer. The point of planning out your time is that you will know if you are taking way too long on each passage- or if you are unnecessarily rushing.

- Make a chart with your halfway point and finish time before you begin the section
- This chart is a rough guideline- not an absolute schedule

Step #2- Prioritize Passages

Take a quick look at your passages. In general, do your non-fiction first, then your fiction, then poetry last (if there is any poetry). If there are any passages that stick out as being really long, save those for last as well. As long as you stay on track with the timing of other passages, you can use your extra time at the end to finish these passages.

- Save really long passages for last
- Save poetry passage for the end

The following are some of the types of passages that you may see:

- *Arts*- These passages may give you a brief biography of an artist or talk about the development of a certain type of art. These tend to be pretty straightforward, so look for them to answer early in the section.

  - Answer arts passages toward the beginning of the section

- *Science*- These passages describe some scientific phenomenon or advancement in the medical field. No need to worry about deep implying or inferring questions here- we won't be asked what the stethoscope was feeling! These are good passages to answer early on.

  - Answer science passages toward the beginning of the section

- *Native culture*- These passages describe some aspect or ritual of a native culture, whether it be Native American, Australian aboriginal, or some other group. Because they are also non-fiction, they tend to be more straightforward, so prioritize these passages.

  - Answer native cultures passages toward the beginning of the section

- *History*- These non-fiction passages tell about a particular era in history. Like our other non-fiction passages, these are good to answer early.

  - Answer history passages toward the beginning

- *Primary Document*- These passages provide part of a document that was written during a different period in history. Generally, they come from American history, so you may see part of a speech by Abraham Lincoln, or a newspaper account from the First World War. These are a little less straightforward. Technically, no knowledge of the time period is necessary. However, if you know about the background of what the passage addresses, the odds of getting the inferring and implying questions right goes up. With these passages, look for the ones that you know something about but save the others for later.

- If you are familiar with the topic, answer primary document passages earlier in the section; if you are not familiar with the topic, save primary document passages for near the end

- *Essay-* These passages consist of an author writing eloquently about a particular topic or idea. The problem with essays is that they tend to use a lot of metaphor or analogy. Makes them more fun to read, but less fun to try to translate into multiple-choice questions. Save these for toward the end.

  - Save essays for near the end

- *Fiction or Folktale-* A lot of the fiction passages that you see will be folktales. These are generally stories from other cultures that have a moral or lesson as the punchline. Fiction questions tend to be very picky and the correct answer may be found in just a word or two. Fiction passages don't have the same strict organization as other passages, so trying to find the answer can be like looking for a needle in a haystack- while someone times you. Save these for the end.

  - Save fiction or folktale passages for near the end
  - Questions tend to be pickier and organization makes it harder to find the right answer easily

- *Poetry-* If you get a poetry passage, it should be the absolute last passage that you answer. Poetry doesn't exactly lend itself to one size fits all interpretation, but this is a multiple-choice test. Don't be surprised if you find yourself disagreeing with the test writers about the correct answers on these passages. The kicker is that their vote counts and yours does not.

  - If you get a poetry passage, answer it last
  - Hard to turn a poem into good multiple-choice questions

Do you see the trend here? Straightforward non-fiction passages make it easy to pick out the right multiple choice answer. Fiction is a little trickier. And poetry as a multiple choice endeavor? Never a good idea.

- Non fiction = good
- Fiction = less good
- Poetry = iffy at best

In general, you also want to answer passages that interest you most first. You don't want to wear yourself out by dragging your way through a dreadfully boring passage and then be mentally exhausted out for a passage that you do like. For example, if you have more than one non-fiction passage, then you would first answer the one(s) that you find more interesting.

Drill #2

You start the reading section. After a quick scan of each passage, you have to prioritize the order of answering the passages. Quickly number the passages below in the order that you would answer them.

Number passages 1-7 with 1 being the first passage you would answer and 7 being the last passage you would answer.

Passage topics:

Native American folktale about how people got fire: #_____

Poem: #_____

Passage about the invention of the unicycle: #_____

News article from World War I: #_____

Traditional tale from China: #_____

Passage about why we have Leap Day: #_____

Passage from a novel #_____

(Please see end of reading comprehension section for answers)

Step #3- When you start a passage, go to questions first

It is important that you identify specific (S) and general (G) questions before you begin to read. You may come across the answer to a specific question as you read, so you also want to underline what the question is asking about for specific questions.

- Mark questions S or G

- For specific questions, underline the key word that it is asking about

So how do you know if it is specific or general?

Here are some examples of the form that specific questions often take:
- In the first paragraph, the word _____ means
- In line 5, _____ means
- In line 7, _____ most likely refers to
- All of the following are mentioned EXCEPT
- All of the following questions are answered EXCEPT

If there is a line reference or the question has a lot of details in it, then it is probably a specific question.

If there is a line reference, go ahead and put a mark next to that line in the passage. That way you will know to go answer that question when you are reading. If the question asks about a specific detail, underline what it asks about so that you know what to look for when you read.

- If there is a line reference, mark that line reference in the passage
- If the question asks about a specific detail, underline that detail in the question so that you know what to look for when you read

For example, let's say our question was:

1. How many years did it take Johnny Appleseed to plant his trees?

   We would underline the word "years" since that is the detail we are looking for. Presumably, the whole passage would be about him planting trees so that would not be a helpful detail to look for.

Some questions may look general, but on the SSAT they are looking for a specific example.

Here is how these questions may look:

- The author would most likely agree
- Which of the following questions is answered by the passage?
- According to the passage/author
- It can be inferred from the passage
- This passage infers/implies which of the following

The reason that these questions are specific is that on the SSAT the answer to these question types will be found in a single sentence or two. In real life, that may not be true, but on this test, it is. We can't underline anything for these questions, however, since the details we are looking for are in the answer choices.

- In real life, these questions might not be specific, but on the SSAT they are
- Nothing to underline since it is the answer choices that give details and not the questions

General questions ask about the passage as a whole.

They might look like:
- This passage primarily deals with
- This passage is mainly about
- What is the best title of this passage?
- The author's tone is

If you see the words "main" or "primary" you have a general question on your hands and should mark it with a G.

Please keep in mind that you do not have to be correct every time when you mark S or G. Do not obsess over whether a question is specific or general. The point of this strategy is to save you time and it just isn't that big of a deal if you mark one question incorrectly.

- Mark S or G quickly- not a big deal if you get it wrong

Below are some practice drills for identifying specific and general questions. Mark each question as specific or general. If the question is specific, then underline the key word or phrase that you would look for in the passage.

Time yourself on each drill so that you can see your improvement- and how easy it is to do this quickly! And remember, absolute accuracy is not a must. If we obsess over correctly labeling the questions S or G, then we won't save ourselves any time.

For the following drills:

- Mark S or G

- Underline what the question is looking for if it is specific

Drill #3

1. This passage is primarily about

2. As used in line 7, "graciously" most nearly means

3. It can be inferred from the passage that all of the following statements about types of grasses are correct EXCEPT

4. According to the passage, how long did it take to travel across the country on the first transcontinental railway?

5. The author's style is best described as

Time:

Drill #4

1. The door to the barn was probably made from

2. The sounds referred to in the passage were

3. According to the author, the musicians stopped playing because

4. An "emu" is probably a type of

5. The mood of this passage can best be described as

Time:

(Answers to drills are found at the end of the reading comprehension section)

Drill #5

1. The sound that came from the floorboards can best be described as

2. It can be inferred that from the passage that earlier settlers did not have windows in their homes because

3. What made the citizens call a town meeting?

4. As it is used in line 15, the word substantial most nearly means

5. Which of the following questions is answered by information in the passage?

Time:

Drill #6

1. Which of the following best state the main idea of the passage?

2. In line 4, John Adams' use of the word "furious" is ironic for which of the following reasons?

3. How does Adams' speech reflect the idea that government is "for the people, by the people"?

4. The purpose of Adams' speech was to

5. Why does Adams use the word "mocking" in line 13?

Time:

(Answers to drills are found at the end of the reading comprehension section)

Step #4- Read the passage

Now, you can go ahead and read the passage. If you happen to run across the answer to one of your specific questions, go ahead and answer it. If not, don't stress about it.

You have to be a little zen about looking for the answers while you read. You can spend five minutes obsessing over finding the answer for one particular question, but if you just move on, you are likely to come across the answer later.

- It's a little like love, sometimes you just have to let it go and trust that it will come back to you

Step #5- Answer specific questions

After you finish reading, answer any specific questions that you have not yet answered. For these questions, think of it as a treasure hunt. The right answer is there, you just have to find it. Generally, you should be able to underline the exact answer paraphrased in the passage. If you can't do that, you just haven't found it yet. Keep looking. You should also think about whether or not the question fits into a particular category (we will work on those in just a minute).

When you are looking for the answer to a specific question, skim! Don't read every word, you have already done that. Look quickly for the words that you underlined in the question. Also, remember our old friend ruling out.

- Skim when looking for the answers for specific questions
- Use ruling out
- For specific questions, you should underline the correct answer restated in the passage
- Look for questions that fit into a particular category of questions

Here are five categories of specific questions that you may see on the SSAT:

- Meaning
- Questions that look general but are really specific
- Inferred/Implied
- EXCEPT

- Tone or attitude about a specific topic

(There are many more specific questions that do not fall into a particular category. Just keep in mind that you want to underline the correct answer in the passage for any specific questions).

Meaning Questions

These questions ask you to identify the meaning of a word or statement. There are several different ways that the test writers might phrase this kind of question.

How they might look:

- In the first paragraph, the word _____ means
- Which word is closest in meaning to _____?
- Which word could be substituted for _____ without changing the meaning?

These questions aren't hard if you use our approach! Here is what you do:

- First locate the reference in the passage
- Then cross out the reference in the passage
- Plug in answer choices and see what makes the most sense

The trick for meaning questions is not to be afraid of words that you don't know.
Rule out what you know doesn't work, and if you have to guess, don't shy away from a word just because you aren't sure what it means. Remember how test writers have to make sure that not everyone is getting a perfect score? Well, students HATE to guess words that they are unsure of the meaning of. So the correct answer on these types of questions is often a word that you do not know.

- Don't shy away from a word that you do not know

Following is a sample passage. Use this passage to answer all of the drills for the specific question types. This book is designed so that you can tear out the passage instead of flipping back and forth. Be sure to do this so that you can develop good habits such as:

- Underline correct answers in the passage for specific questions
- Use ruling out- physically cross out answer choices that do not work

Use the passage on the following page to answer the questions.

Drill #7

1. When the author mentions "thoroughfares" in the first paragraph she is referring to
   (A) the driver
   (B) London
   (C) the cab that Sarah is riding in
   (D) roads
   (E) passengers

2. As used in the first sentence of the passage, the word "blazed" most nearly means
   (A) darkened
   (B) shone
   (C) froze
   (D) limited
   (E) focused

(Answers to drills are found at the end of the reading comprehension section)

This page left intentionally blank so that passage can be removed from book to use for drills.

Passage for specific questions drills:

Once on a dark winter's day, when the yellow fog hung so thick and heavy in the streets of London that the lamps were lighted and the shop windows blazed with gas as they do at night, an odd-looking little girl sat in a cab with her father and was driven rather slowly through the big thoroughfares.

She sat with her feet tucked under her, and leaned against her father, who held her in his arm, as she stared out of the window at the passing people with a queer old-fashioned thoughtfulness in her big eyes.

She was such a little girl that one did not expect to see such a look on her small face. It would have been an old look for a child of twelve, and Sara Crewe was only seven. The fact was, however, that she was always dreaming and thinking odd things and could not herself remember any time when she had not been thinking things about grown-up people and the world they belonged to. She felt as if she had lived a long, long time.

This page left intentionally blank so that passage
can be removed from book to use for drills.

Questions that look general but are really specific

On the SSAT, there will be questions that if you saw them outside of this test, you would think they were asking about the passage in general. Because we are experts on the SSAT, however, we know that these questions are really looking for a detail.

The answer can generally be found in a single sentence

These questions might look like:

- The author would most likely agree
- Which of the following questions is answered by the passage?
- According to the passage/author
- The setting of the story is

Our approach to these questions is just like any other specific question. The trick to these questions is not in how to answer them, but rather in recognizing them in the first place. You may be asking why a question about setting would be specific. The reason is that the answer is often given in just a sentence or small phrase.

- You should be able to underline the correct answer
- Skim, skim, skim until you find the answer- it is often only one word
- Use ruling out—a lot

Tricks for questions that look general but are specific:

- The test writers often take a sentence from the passage and twist it around to mean something different- just make sure you can underline the answer in the passage
- You might think they are looking for a general theme, but they are usually looking for just one or two words

Below are a couple of sample questions. They refer back to the passage about Sara.

Drill #8

1. Which of the following statements would the author most likely agree with?
   (A) Sarah was twelve years old.
   (B) It was not safe to go on a drive on that particular day.
   (C) Sarah was smaller than other children her age.
   (D) Sarah seemed much older than she actually was.
   (E) Sarah's father is unusual looking.

2. Which of the following questions is answered by the passage?
   (A) In what city does this story take place?
   (B) In what year does this story take place?
   (C) Where were Sarah and her father going?
   (D) Did Sarah have any siblings?
   (E) Where did Sarah live?

(Answers to drills are found at the end of the reading comprehension section)

Inferred/Implied Questions

These questions make you think that you should be reading deeply into the passage. This is not the case, however.

Perhaps the passage says:

"The boy hung his head and held back the tears as he brushed the sand from his feet."

The question then asks:

Which of the following was implied by the passage?
(A) the boy was sad and upset that his friends did not include him
(B) completely unrelated answer
(C) the boy had just returned from the beach
(D) completely unrelated answer
(E) completely unrelated answer

You have ruled out three answer choices and are down to choices A and C. In school, you are expected to read into passages and look for emotions when there is an implied question, so it is tempting to select choice A. However, this is the SSAT and there is no evidence that he was sad BECAUSE his friends did not include him. However, he is brushing sand off of this feet, so we can assume that he was in a sandy place such as the beach. The context of the rest of the passage would matter, but the general idea is that we are not looking for deep emotions, but rather more literal answers.

- When debating between two answer choices, look for the more literal answer choice

These questions can look like:
- It can be inferred from the passage
- This passage infers/implies which of the following

To approach these questions:
- Don't do too much thinking of your own. While the words infer and imply suggest that you should be making your own leaps of thought and conclusions, they are really just looking for something paraphrased from the passage.
- These are still specific questions so we are looking to underline an answer

Tricks for implying or inferring questions:
- The answer can often be found in just a few words and is not a main idea.

Complete the following drill. The question refers back to the passage about Sara.

Drill #9

1. Which of the following can be inferred from the passage?
   (A) Sarah was an unhappy child.
   (B) The driver of the cab was driving cautiously.
   (C) Sarah did not like her father.
   (D) London was a very large city.
   (E) Sarah did not live with her mother.

(Answers to drills are found at the end of the reading comprehension section)

EXCEPT/NOT Questions

How they might look:

- All of the following are mentioned EXCEPT
- All of the following questions are answered EXCEPT
- Which of the following is NOT true?

How to approach:

- Circle the word EXCEPT or NOT- even though they put them in all caps, it is really easy to forget once you start looking for an answer
- For these questions, you should be able to underline four of the answers in the passage- it is the answer that you cannot underline that is the correct one
- After you underline an answer in the passage, cross out that answer choice so that you don't choose it by mistake!

Tricks for EXCEPT questions:

- Students tend to just forget the EXCEPT or NOT!

The following drill refers back to the Persephone passage.

1. All of the following are mentioned in the passage EXCEPT
   (A) winter weather in London
   (B) Sarah's personality
   (C) Sarah's father's personality
   (D) how shop lights were powered in London at the time of this story
   (E) Sarah's physical appearance

Tone or Attitude About a Specific Topic Questions

There are two types of tone and attitude questions. One type asks you about the author's tone or attitude in general, and one type asks what the author feels about a particular subject. It is that second type that we will focus on here.

These questions may look like:

- The author's tone regarding _____ is
- The author's attitude about _____ is

Here is our approach for these tone and attitude questions that ask about only a small part of the passage:

- Locate the part of the passage that discusses this topic
- Stick to this area while you rule out answer choices

Tricks to look out for with tone or attitude questions:

- Rule out answers that are too extreme, in a positive or negative way
- Don't be afraid of words you don't know

Please complete the drill below. The question refers back to the passage about Sara.

1. Which of the following describes the author's tone about winter weather in London?
    (A) dreary
    (B) hopeful
    (C) defensive
    (D) enthusiastic
    (E) inquisitive

Step #6- Answer general questions

After answering the specific questions, you have probably reread the passage multiple times. The trick for the general questions is not to get bogged down by the details, however. How do we do this? By rereading the last sentence of the entire passage before we answer general questions. This will clarify the main idea.

- Reread last sentence of passage before answering general questions

General questions are those that are about the passage as a whole, and not just a specific part of the passage.

There are 4 main types:
- Main Idea
- Tone or Attitude
- Organization
- Style

Main Idea Questions

Main idea questions are looking for you to identify what the passage is about. You can identify them because they often use the words main or primarily.

- Often have the words "main" or "primarily" in them

Here is what they may look like:

- This passage primarily deals with
- The main purpose of this passage is to
- Which of the following best expresses the author's main point?
- What is the best title of this passage?

How to approach main idea questions:

- Reread the last sentence of the entire passage and look for the answer that comes closest to this sentence

Tricks to look out for with main idea questions:

- Answers that give details from the passage but are not the main idea

Usually, the wrong answers are mentioned in the passage, but they are incorrect because they are not the main idea.

Following is a passage to be used for all the general question practice drills. The book is designed so that you can tear out the page instead of flipping pages while trying to answer questions.

Please complete the following drill using the Hantavirus passage on the following page.

Drill #12

1. What is the main idea of this passage?
   (A) the symptoms of the hantavirus
   (B) the history of the hantavirus
   (C) the history of Yosemite Park
   (D) a recent outbreak of the hantavirus at Yosemite
   (E) how the hantavirus is spread

2. Which of the following would be the best title for this passage?
   (A) Terror at Yosemite Park
   (B) An outbreak of a virus at Yosemite
   (C) A brief history of the hantavirus
   (D) Summertime blues
   (E) The dangers of hiking in national parks

Passage for general questions drills

Many recent visitors to Yosemite National Park have been diagnosed with Hantavirus Pulmonary Syndrome. The disease is caused by infected mice, and in particular, deer mice. Exposure to the mouse feces or urine could result in human infection.

California Department of Public Health and Yosemite National Park Public Health Service officers conduct routine inspections and monitor rodent activity and mouse populations. Park officials also actively perform rodent proofing inspections of all facilities and buildings throughout the park.

The CDPH recommended the park increase rodent control measures to reduce the risk of exposing visitors to the hantavirus. Extra inspections, more thorough cleaning of the cabins, and increased overall sanitation measures have been implemented to discourage mouse infestations.

Symptoms of the disease usually appear between one and six weeks after exposure and are similar to those of influenza, including fever, headaches, and muscle aches. The infection progresses rapidly into severe breathing problems and sometimes death. Because of these severe consequences, the park rangers at Yosemite have taken the current outbreak of Hantavirus very seriously and are working to let visitors know who might have been affected.

This page left intentionally blank so that passage can be removed from book to use for drills.

Tone or Attitude Questions

Previously, we worked on tone and attitude questions that were about a particular topic. These tone and attitude questions refer to the entire passage.

They might look like this:

- The author's tone is
- The author's attitude is

If the question does not refer to a specific part of the passage, you can assume that it applies to the passage as a whole.

How to approach:

- Reread the last sentence of the passage
- Use ruling out

Tricks to look out for with tone or attitude questions:

- Rule out answers that are too extreme, in a positive or negative way
- Don't be afraid of words you don't know
- Think about the type of passage that you are reading (fiction or non-fiction)
- Non-fiction passages tend to have correct answers that are like the words objective, informative, interested, etc.
- Fiction passages tend to have more emotional answers such as nervous, excited, determined, etc.

The following drill refers back to the passage about hantavirus at Yosemite.

Drill #13

1. The author's tone can best be described as
   (A) disappointed
   (B) ambivalent
   (C) jealous
   (D) outraged
   (E) informative

(Answers to drills are found at the end of the reading comprehension section)

Organization questions

Some questions require you to think about the organization of the passage a whole.

They might look something like this:

- Which of the following will the author discuss next?
- What will (name of a character) do next?

To approach these questions:

- Next to each paragraph, label in a word or two what it is talking about
- Use these labels to look for a natural flow in what would come next

Tricks to look out for on organization questions:

- Answers that repeat the main idea of another paragraph - the author is not likely to repeat themselves
- Answers that relate to the main idea, but are pretty far removed or are a much broader topic than the passage

The following drill refers back to the passage about hantavirus at Yosemite.

Drill #14

1. Which of the following is the author most likely to discuss next?
   (A) where the hantavirus was first discovered
   (B) the history of outbreaks at other parks
   (C) what park rangers at Yosemite have learned from this outbreak
   (D) how viruses change over time
   (E) the future of vaccines

(Answers to drills are found at the end of the reading comprehension section)

Style Questions

These questions ask you to identify where you might find a passage.

They might look like:

- What is the style of the passage?
- This passage can best be described as
- The answer choices will give different types of writing such as a newspaper article, propaganda, a manual, etc.

How to approach:

- First, ask yourself if it is fiction or non-fiction. If it is fiction, rule out any non-fiction forms. If it is non-fiction, then rule out any fiction forms.
- If it is more scholarly non-fiction (i.e. dry and boring) , then the correct answer is likely to be something like a textbook or encyclopedia entry.
- If it is non-fiction but still telling a story, it might be an account of an event, a news article or item, or found in a newspaper.
- If they are trying to persuade the reader, then it could be propaganda (selling an idea) or an advertisement (selling a product).
- Fiction passages tend to be found either in a novel or in some sort of anthology.

Tricks for style questions:

- Any form of writing that is too technical won't show up on this test (medical journals, manuals, etc.)

The following drill refers back to the passage about hantavirus.

Drill #15

1. Where would this passage most likely be found?
   (A) a personal diary
   (B) a newspaper
   (C) a diagnosis manual
   (D) correspondence between two physicians
   (E) a novel

(Answers to drills are found at the end of the reading comprehension section)

Step #7- Move on to your next passage and repeat!

When you complete a passage, check your time against the chart your created before starting the section and then move on to the next passage.

- Keep track of time
- Just keep on truckin'

Secrets for helping you choose the type of answer that test writers prefer

Ruling out is particularly important on the reading section. Often, you will read through the answer choices and right away you can rule out two or three answer choices.

The art of answering reading questions correctly comes down to three things:

- Look for answer choices that are harder to argue with
- Watch out for answer choices that take words from the passage and move them around so that the meaning is different
- Be careful not to let your brain fill in details that are not there

Secret #1: Look for answer choices that are harder to argue with.

The people who write the SSAT have to make sure that there is no dispute over what the correct answer is to a question.

How do they do this? When they write a question, they come up with five answer choices. Then they go back and make sure that four of those answer choices have something in them that makes them wrong. Those are the details that we want to look for!

Basically, when you are debating between two answer choices, ask yourself which one is easiest to make a case against. Rule that one out.

- Four answer choices for every question have something that makes them wrong
- Wrong answer choices are easier to argue with
- Rule out the answer choices that are easier to argue with

So what is it that makes an answer choice easy to argue with?

1. Extreme words
2. Words that leave no room for negotiation (always, never, all, etc.)

What are extreme words?

Think of words existing on a spectrum. Words in the middle are pretty neutral, but words on either end are extreme.

Here is an example:

Let's say you were looking for a word to describe your experience with the latest phone app. Here is one possible range of the words that you might use:

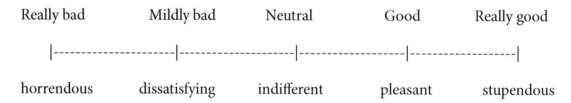

Horrendous and stupendous would be really extreme words, so they would not likely be the right answer choice on the SSAT. They are too easy to argue with. The words dissatisfying, indifferent, and pleasant, however, are more in the middle. It is harder to argue with them, so they are more likely to be correct on the SSAT.

- When you are trying to decide whether a word is extreme, think of where it would fall on a spectrum compared to other words with a similar meaning

To complete the following drill, rule out answer choices that are too extreme and choose from what is left. Yes, there is no passage! The point here is to use your knowledge of the type of answer choices that are preferred in order to answer the question.

Answer the following drill using just what you know about what types of answers tend to be right on the SSAT.

1. The author's attitude toward juvenile imprisonment can be described best as one of
    (A) hostile attack
    (B) enthusiastic support
    (C) sarcastic criticism
    (D) jubilant support
    (E) cautious optimism

2. Which of the following phrases would the author use to describe George Washington?
    (A) Triumphant warrior
    (B) Vile wretch
    (C) Committed patriot
    (D) Untalented ruler
    (E) Tyrant

(Answers for all drills are given at the end of the reading section)

Which words leave no room for negotiation?

Words such as always, never, and all are too easy to argue with. Let's say that I tell you that the bus is always late. That would be a really easy statement to argue with. If the bus was on time even once, then I would be wrong because I used the word always. Let's say that I tell you

Abraham Lincoln never thought that the union would actually break apart. How could I possibly know that? A correct answer would say something like "there is no evidence that Abraham Lincoln thought that the union might break apart" rather than "Abraham Lincoln never thought the union would break apart."

- Words such as all, none, entirely, always, never, and all are too easy to argue with

For the following drill, pretend that you are down to two answer choices. You have ruled out the other three as definitely incorrect and now you have to choose the answer choice that is hardest to argue with. Circle the one that you would choose on the actual test.

Drill #17

Choice 1: Asteroids never hit the Earth.
Choice 2: Scientists have not observed an asteroid colliding with the earth.

Choice 1: The facts of the story all point to the same conclusion.
Choice 2: The story is described in a way that suggests one conclusion.

Choice 1: No sailors were found on the decks of the ship.
Choice 2: None of the sailors survived the storm.

Choice 1: The basketball players were disappointed by the loss.
Choice 2: All of the basketball players left the game upset because of the loss.

(Answers to drills are found at the end of the reading comprehension section)

Secret #2: Watch out for answer choices that take words from the passage and move them around so that the meaning is different.

On the SSAT, answer choices often have words from the passage. More often than not, however, these words are twisted around so that the meaning is different. Usually the right answer choice has synonyms for words in the passage. That doesn't mean you should rule out all choices that repeat words from the passage, it just means that you should be careful when words are repeated from the passage.

- Be cautious when choosing an answer that repeats words from the passage

Here is an example:

Let's say that the passage states:

John was upset when Sam got into the car with Trish.

The question may look something like:

1. Which of the following is implied by the author?
   (A) John was upset with Trish when Sam got into the car
   (B) John was upset with Trish when he got into the car
   (C) Sam and Trish were upset when John got into the car
   (D) John and Sam were cousins
   (E) John was not happy because Sam rode with Trish

Answer choices A, B, and C all use words from the passage, but do not have the same meaning as what the passage says. Choice D is just unrelated- which happens on the SSAT! Choice E restates the passage without using exact words from the passage.

In the drill below, there is a sentence from a passage. There is then a list of answer choices. You have to decide whether the answer choice has the same meaning as the passage, or whether the words have been twisted around to mean something else.

Drill #18

Passage 1: After being persuaded by the pleading of Father Thomas O'Reilly, when Sherman ordered the city of Atlanta burned, he spared the city's hospitals and churches.

Answer states:	Same meaning	Twisted meaning
1. When Sherman burned the city of Atlanta, only Father Thomas O'Reilly's church was spared.		
2. Atlanta's hospitals and churches were not ordered to be burned by Sherman.		
3. When Atlanta was burned, due to the influence of Father Thomas O'Reilly the city's churches and hospitals remained standing.		
4. Sherman ordered that Atlanta's hospitals and churches not be spared, despite the pleadings of Father Thomas O'Reilly.		

Passage 2: When the morning sun rose high above the horizon, a small boy could be spotted as he carried a bucket along the ridge of a hill in the distance.

Answer states:	Same meaning	Twisted meaning
1. A small boy was spotted along the horizon, looking almost like a bucket on the hill.		
2. Along the ridge, a child was carrying a pail in the morning.		
3. The small boy spotted the sun rising over a ridge as he carried a bucket.		
4. Far away, it was possible to see a boy carrying a bucket as he walked along the top of a hill in the morning sun.		

Secret #3: Be careful not to let your brain fill in details that are not there

As we read, we automatically fill in details. However, the writers of the test know this and use this against you! Remember, the average student is missing a whole lot of reading comprehension questions, despite the fact that he or she probably knows how to read just fine.

For example, let's say that the passage says:

"Samuel came from a family of enormous height- it was said that even his mother was six feet four inches tall."

Look at the following question and decide what answer choice would be a trap (we don't have enough information to pick out the right answer, we are just trying to identify the trick answer).

1. Which of the following about Samuel can be inferred from the passage?
   (A) That he is well educated
   (B) That he is very tall
   (C) His favorite pastime is basketball
   (D) He left school at an early age
   (E) He was the first astronaut to be a pet owner

As we read, our mind probably filled in that Samuel is tall since the passage says that his family was tall. However, the passage does NOT say that Samuel is tall. Odds are good that we won't remember this, however, since our mind has already filled in the blank. The test writers know this and throw in choice B as a trick. This is exactly how they get proficient readers to miss so many questions!

So how do we overcome this trick? By underlining the evidence in the passage for each answer choice for specific questions. Do not go on what you remember- if you can't underline it, it isn't the right answer choice.

- Underlining the evidence for the correct answer choice will keep you from choosing an answer where your brain has drawn its own conclusions

Also watch out for assigning emotions to other people. Let's say a story tells us that a little boy lost his dog. You might assume that he would be sad and choose an answer choice that indicates that. But maybe he always hated that dog! Unless there is evidence of a particular emotion, don't assume that the character would think or feel what you would think or feel.

- Don't assume what a character would feel, there has to be concrete evidence of that emotion

For the following drill, read the passage and then answer the question that follows. Remember to look out for our tricks!

Drill #19

On a dark night, when there was no moon in the sky, a peddler pulled into an inn. He had come from very far away with wares to sell. When the peddler told the innkeeper why he was travelling, the innkeeper was distrustful. He had heard of peddlers and the tricks they liked to play. He said to the peddler, "I will give you a room tonight, but in the morning I want you to show me one of your tricks for which you are so famous." The peddler wearily agreed. He stowed his nag for the night and barely made it to his room upstairs before falling asleep. In the morning, the peddler was feeling much better. As the innkeeper walked through the breakfast room, he saw the peddler talking with the innkeeper's wife and showing her a quilt that matched one that the inn already had. The wife was quite excited as she was in need of another quilt. She counted out the coins for the quilt and the peddler was soon on his way once more. As he drove away, the innkeeper yelled after him, "Hey! I thought you were going to show me one of your famous tricks!" The peddler replied, "I just did. I just sold your wife the quilt off of your own bed."

1. From the passage, which of the following can be inferred?
   (A) the innkeeper was furious at the peddler
   (B) the peddler was tired after his long journey
   (C) the innkeeper's wife was in charge off all the money in the inn
   (D) the quilt on the innkeeper's bed was worn out
   (E) there were no other guests at the inn that night

Now you know what you need to in order to excel on the reading section!

Answers to Drills

Drill #1

Start- 9:32
Halfway point- 9:52, 4 passages
Finish- 10:12

Start- 8:56
Halfway point- 9:16, 3.5 passages
Finish- 9:36

Drill #2

There is not an absolute right order to answer these passages. The passage about the invention of the unicycle, the news article from WWI, and the passage about why we have Leap Day are all non-fiction, so they should have been in your top 3. Your order will vary depending upon what you find interesting! The Native American folktale, the traditional tale from China, and the novel passage should have been #4-6. Again, their exact order will depend on what looked good to you. The poem should be answered last. Always.

Drill #3

1. G
2. S
3. S
4. S
5. G

Drill #4

1. S
2. S
3. S
4. S
5. G

Drill #5

1. S
2. S
3. S
4. S
5. S

You might be asking yourself, would there really be a passage with all specific questions? There could be!

Drill #6

1. G
2. S
3. S or G- it depends on what the whole passage is about. Remember, we have to stay flexible when we do this.
4. G
5. S

Drill #7

1. D
2. B

Drill #8

1. E
2. A

Drill #9

1. B

Drill #10

1. C

Drill #11

1. A

Drill #12

1. D

2. B

Drill #13

1. E

Drill #14

1. C

Drill #15

1. B

Drill #16

1. E
2. C

Drill #17

1. Choice 2
2. Choice 2
3. Choice 1
4. Choice 1

Drill #18

Passage 1:
1. twisted meaning
2. same meaning
3. same meaning
4. twisted meaning

Passage 2:
1. twisted meaning
2. same meaning
3. twisted meaning
4. same meaning

Drill #19

1. B

Quantitative Sections- Basic Strategies

On the quantitative sections, there are problems from arithmetic, algebra, and geometry. The math is really not that hard. The SSAT is more about figuring out what concepts they are testing rather than remembering complicated equations.

- SSAT is more about figuring out what they are testing than hard math

You will NOT be allowed to use a calculator on the SSAT. Yes, you read that correctly. By using strategies, however, we can get to the right answers, often without using complicated calculations.

- No calculator allowed

The goal here is for you to get a general understanding of the key strategies for the math section. Following the basic strategies are content lessons where you will get to apply these new strategies.

Drumroll, please! The strategies are:
- Use estimating- this is a multiple choice test!
- If there are variables in the answer choices, try plugging in your own numbers
- If they ask for the value of a variable, plug in answer choices

Strategy #1: Use Estimating

You can spend a lot of time finding the exact right answer on this test, or you can spend time figuring out what answers couldn't possibly work and then choose from what is left.

For example, let's say the question is:

1.   Which addition problem is closest to 49+31+28?
     (A) 50+30+20
     (B) 50+40+30
     (C) 50+30+30
     (D) 40+30+30
     (E) 40+30+20

If you were to do out the first addition problem and then do each of the sums in the answer choices, that would take a long time without a calculator. However, if we look at our answer choices, we can see that they are not asking us to do the actual addition! They just want to see if we know how to round off in order to estimate. Answer choice C is correct.

You can use estimating on many of the problems, but in particular estimate when the question uses the words "closest to" or "approximately". If you are not sure of how to round off in order to estimate, be sure to read the next section carefully.

Rules for Rounding

Is the number 78 closer to the number 70 or 80? If you said 80, you have a good idea of how rounding works. You have rounded 78 to the nearest 10, which is 80.

Now, what if you are to round a decimal number, like 3.43 to the nearest whole number? Would it be closer to 3 or to 4? The answer is that it is closer to 3. The special name for the "4" of the number 3.43 is the "rounding digit." Notice that when you round down, you drop the rounding digit and all the digits to its right.

Now that you see how rounding works, here are the rules:

- Round down if the rounding digit is 0, 1, 2, 3, or 4. This means to drop the rounding digit and all digits to its right.

For example, rounding 41.278543 to the nearest whole number means that the rounding digit is 2. Since 2 is less than 5, you will round down, meaning that you will drop the rounding digit 2 and all the numbers to its right. So 41.278543 will round to just plain 41.

- Round up if the rounding digit is 5, 6, 7, 8, or 9. This means to make the number to the left of the rounding digit one unit higher, and then drop the rounding digit and all the digits to its right.

For example, if we round the number 46.81 to the nearest whole number then the rounding digit is 8. It is five or greater, so you will round up. This means that the number 46.81 will be rounded up to 47.

Here are some other examples, with the rounding digit underlined:

Rounding to a whole number- The number 3.<u>5</u> is rounded up to 4.

Rounding to the nearest tenth- The number 2.7<u>3</u>22, rounded to the nearest tenth, will be 2.7. Look at the rounding digit, which is 3, and you see that you will round down. So drop the rounding digit and all the digits to its right, and you are left with 2.7.

Below are some questions that show how rounding is tested on the SSAT.

Drill #1

1. The sum 78+52+29 is approximately
   (A) 70+50+20
   (B) 70+60+20
   (C) 70+50+30
   (D) 80+50+30
   (E) 80+60+30

2. Which difference is closest to 5.97−3?
   (A) 5−3
   (B) 6−3
   (C) 60−3
   (D) 600−3
   (E) 500−3

(Please check the end of math strategy section for answers to drills. They are located at the end of the strategies section but before the content material.)

Strategy #2: Plug in your own numbers if there are variables in the answer choices

What do I mean by variables in the answer choices? If you look at the answer choices and some or all of them have letters in addition to numbers, then you have variables in your answer choices.

- Look for letters in the answer choices

Here is how this strategy works:

1. Make up your own numbers for the variables

Just make sure they work within the problem. If they say that x is less than 1, do not make x equal to 2! If they say $x + y = 1$, then for heavens sake, don't make x equal to 2 and y equal to 3. Also, make sure that you write down what you are plugging in for your variables. EVERY TIME. You think you will remember that x was 4, but then you go to try out answer choices and it gets all confused. Just write it down the first time. Also, try to avoid using -1, 1, and 0 because they have funky properties and you might get more than one answer that works. The exception to this rule is when the question asks you what must be true. In that case, you want to use the funky numbers to try to rule out answer choices.

2. Solve the problem using your numbers

Write down the number that you get and circle it. This is the number you are trying to get with your answer choices when you plug in your value for the variable.

3. Plug the numbers that you assigned to the variables in step 1 into the answer choices and see which answer choice matches the number that you circled.

Here is an example:

1. Suzy has q more pencils than Jim. If Jim has 23 pencils, then how many pencils does Suzy have?
   (A) $q/23$
   (B) $q - 23$
   (C) $q + 23$
   (D) $23 - q$
   (E) $23/q$

Step 1: Plug in our own number.

Let's make q equal to 4. Suzy now has 4 more pencils than Jim.

Step 2: Solve using our own numbers.

If Jim has 23 pencils, and Suzy has four more than Jim, then Suzy must have 27 pencils. This is our target. Circle it. 27 is the number that we want to get when we plug in 4 for q in our answer choices.

Step 3: Plug into answer choices.

1. We are looking for the answer choice that would be equal to 27.

    (A) $q/23 = 4/23$

    (B) $q - 23 = 4 - 23 = -19$

    (C) $q + 23 = 4 + 23 = 27$

    (D) $23 - q = 23 - 4 = 19$

    (E) $23/q = 23/4$

Choice C gives us 27, which is what we were looking for, so we choose C and get the question correct.

If the question asks you which answer choice is greatest or least, then you won't come up with a target number to circle. Rather, you will just plug your values into the answer choices and see which one is greatest or least, depending on what the question asked for.

*   If question asks which answer choice is greatest or least, you won't come up with a target, you will just plug into answer choices

Here is an example:

1. Two times which number is greatest?

    (A) $X + 2$

    (B) $X - 2$

    (C) X

    (D) $X + 1$

    (E) $X - 1$

Step 1: Choose our own numbers.

Let's make X equal to 2. This is a nice, easy number to work with

Step 2: Solve using our own numbers.

For this kind of problem, we skip step 2. There is no target since we are looking to compare answer choices.

Step 3: Plug into answer choices and then multiply by 2 (since the question asks "two times which number") and see what gives us the GREATEST number

    (A) $X + 2 = 2 + 2 = 4 \times 2 = 8$
    (B) $X - 2 = 2 - 2 = 0 \times 2 = 0$
    (C) $X = 2 \times 2 = 4$
    (D) $X + 1 = 2 + 1 = 3 \times 2 = 6$
    (E) $X - 1 = 2 - 1 = 1 \times 2 = 2$

By plugging in our own numbers, we can clearly see that choice A gives us the GREATEST number, so we choose choice A and get it right!

Another problem type that has variables in the answer choices is questions that ask what "must be true". For these questions, plug in your own numbers and rule out any answer choices that don't work for your numbers. If there is more than one answer choice that works, then just pick different numbers. Since it is a "must be true" problem, the correct answer choice has to work with ALL numbers. If you need to, just keep picking new numbers until you have only one answer choice that has not been ruled out.

- With "must be true" problems, if you have ruled out all that you can but there is more than one answer choice left, just pick new numbers and keep ruling out until there is only one choice left

Here is an example:

1.   If b is 3 more than w, then w must be
    (A) 3
    (B) less than 3
    (C) more than 3
    (D) 3 more than b
    (E) 3 less than b

To solve, let's make b equal to 4. That would make w equal to 1. This allows us to rule out answer choices A, C, and D. However, choices B and E are still in the running. So let's choose another number for b. Let's make b equal to 10. This would make w equal to 7. That is greater than 3, so we can rule out choice B. That leaves us with choice E, which is the correct answer.

Below is another drill to try. To solve these problems, use plugging in your own numbers!

Drill #2

1. If Q is an even number, which answer choices must also be even
   I. $Q + 1$
   II. $Q + 2$
   III. $2Q$
   IV. $3Q$

   (A) I only
   (B) I and II
   (C) II and III
   (D) II, III, and IV
   (E) I, II, III, and IV

2. Sheila had w baseball cards. She gave five cards to Tommy but then she received three cards from Jill. In terms of w, how many cards did Sheila now have?
   (A) $w - 15$
   (B) $w - 8$
   (C) $w - 2$
   (D) $w + 2$
   (E) $w + 5$

3. Charlotte paid for an ice cream cone with a $5 bill. She received d dollars in change. How many dollars did she pay for the ice cream cone?
   (A) $5 + d$
   (B) $5 - d$
   (C) $d - 5$
   (D) $d + 5$
   (E) $5d$

The next three problems are pretty challenging. If you are in fifth (or even 6th) grade, remember that your percentile score is what matters and that score will only compare you to other students your age. So if these problems seem really tough, don't worry about it!

Challenge problems:

4. To ride in a certain taxicab costs X dollars for the first two miles and Y dollars for each additional mile travelled. How much does it cost, in dollars, to ride for 7 miles?

   (A) $X + (5 \times Y)$
   (B) $X + (7 \times Y)$
   (C) $2 \times X + (5 \times Y)$
   (D) $2 \times X + (7 \times Y)$
   (E) $7 \times (X + Y)$

5. K is a number less than 1. If K is multiplied by a positive whole number, then the answer must be which of the following?

   (A) 0
   (B) less than K
   (C) greater than K
   (D) greater than the number K was multiplied by
   (E) less than the number K was multiplied by

6. If the width of a rectangle is 4 times the length, l, which of the following gives the perimeter of the rectangle in terms of l?

   (A) $3l$
   (B) $5l$
   (C) $10l$
   (D) $2(4 + l)$
   (E) $4(4 + l)$

(Please check the end of math strategy section for answers to drills. They are located at the end of the strategies section but before the content material.)

Strategy #3: If they ask for the value of a variable, plug in answer choices

On the SSAT, it is often easier to plug in answer choices and see what works. In particular, you may find this strategy most helpful on word problems. After all, this is a multiple choice test so one of those answers has to work!

- Can often use this strategy on word problems
- This is a multiple choice test!

For this strategy, keep in mind that a variable is not always a letter. The problem might define x as the number of cars, or it might just ask you what the number of cars is. Either way, it is still asking for the value of a variable and you can use this strategy.

- A variable may not always be a letter, it can be any unknown quantity

Whenever a question asks for the value of a variable, whether it is a letter or something like the number of bunnies, one of those answer choices has to work. Since this is a multiple-choice test, you just have to figure out which one. Ruling out is one of our most important strategies and this scenario is just another example of how valuable a tool ruling out can be.

- Remember the mantra: Ruling out is good

Here are the steps for using this strategy:

Step 1: Put your answer choices in order from least to greatest if they are not already in that order (they usually are already in order, but SSATB sometimes mixes things up)

Step 2: Plug the middle answer choice into the problem to see if it works. The exception to this rule is if the question asks what is the smallest number or greatest number. If they ask for the smallest number, start with the smallest number, and if they ask for the greatest number, then start with the largest number.

- Usually we start in middle
- If they ask for the smallest number, start with the smallest number
- If they ask for the greatest number, start with the largest number

Step 3: If the middle choice does not work, go bigger or smaller depending on what you got for the middle answer choice.

Here is an example:

1. If three times a number is 18, what is the number?
    (A) 3
    (B) 6
    (C) 12
    (D) 15
    (E) 18

In this case, the answer choices are already in order (they usually are), so we can skip step 1 and go right to step 2.

Step 2: Plug in middle answer choice.

We make our number equal to answer choice C, which is 12. It says that three times a number is 18, but three times 12 is 36. That means we can rule out answer choice C.

Step 3: Go bigger or smaller if the middle answer choice did not work.

Answer choice C gave us a number that was too big, so we will try choice B next. If we plug in 6, three times 6 would give us 18. That tells us that choice B is correct.

For the following drill, try plugging in answer choices to see what works. Even if you know how to solve another way, you need to practice this strategy because there will be a time when you need it to bail you out.

Drill #3

1. Sam is thinking of a number halfway between 15 and 21. What number is he thinking of?
   (A) 16
   (B) 17
   (C) 18
   (D) 19
   (E) 20

2. If four times a number is 32, what is the number?
   (A) 4
   (B) 8
   (C) 12
   (D) 16
   (E) 128

3. Carol has a jar with pennies, nickels, dimes and quarters in it. She needs to take 57 cents from the jar. What is the least number of coins she can take from the jar and have exactly 57 cents?
   (A) 2
   (B) 3
   (C) 4
   (D) 5
   (E) 7

(Please check your answers for drills at the end of the math strategies section)

Those are the basic strategies that you need to know for the math section. As you go through the content sections, you will learn content and the strategies that work for specific problem types.

Answers to Math Strategies Drills

Drill #1

1. D
2. B

Drill #2

1. D
2. C
3. B
4. A
5. E
6. C

Drill #3

1. C
2. B
3. D

Math Content Sections

We have covered the basic strategies for the math section. Now, we are going to take a look at some of the problem types that you will see on this test.

On the SSAT, sometimes the math to solve a problem is not that hard. However, the tough part of that problem might be recognizing what direction to go and what concept is being tested.

Doing well on the math section is often a matter of decision making. You need to decide what type of problem you are working on as well as what the most efficient way to solve will be.

Each lesson will:

- Teach you the facts that you need to know
- Show you how those facts are tested
- Give you plenty of practice

That is the book's side of the bargain, but you also have to keep up your end of the deal.

As you work through the content always ask yourself:

- What makes this problem unique?
- How will I recognize this problem in the future?

You are on your way to crushing the SSAT math section!

Math Fundamentals

Now let's put the fun in fundamentals.

If you are one of those students who think that math basics are no laughing matter, not to worry. You really don't have to know a lot of definitions or equations. The SSAT is testing your ability to reason and recognize concepts, not your ability to memorize.

This section will teach you what you need to know, just what you need to know, and nothing more.

This section will cover:

- Different kinds of numbers that you need to know
- How to interpret equation/inequality language
- The math facts that you will need to know
- How to square a number or find a square root
- Problems that test different operations
- Place value

Different Kinds of Numbers

On the SSAT, you will need to know what some different kinds of numbers are. They include:

- Integer
- Whole Number
- Positive
- Negative
- Even
- Odd
- Consecutive

Integers and whole numbers are very similar. Simply put, they are numbers that do not have decimals or fractions. For example, 0, 1, 2, and 3 are all integers as well as whole numbers. The difference is that integers include negative numbers. On this test, however, they don't really require you to know the difference between integers and whole numbers. You just need to know that if they ask for an integer or a whole number, the correct answer cannot have a fraction or decimal.

- If they ask for an integer or whole number, no decimals or fractions

Positive numbers are those that are greater than zero. Negative numbers are those that are less than zero. The only tricky thing about positive and negative numbers is that zero is neither positive nor negative. The SSAT is not likely to ask you if zero is positive or negative, but they might tell you that a variable is positive, in which case you have to know that it can't equal zero.

- Zero is neither positive nor negative

Even numbers are those numbers that are evenly divisible by 2. That means that you can divide even numbers into groups of two with nothing left over. Odd numbers are those that cannot be evenly divided by 2. By this definition, zero is an even number because it can be divided by two with nothing left over. Even numbers are 0, 2 4 6, and so on. Odd numbers are 1, 3, 5, and so on.

- Zero is an even number

Consecutive numbers are simply integers that are next to each other when you count. For example, 1 and 2 are consecutive numbers. There are also consecutive even numbers and consecutive odd numbers. These are just the numbers that would be next to each other if you counted by twos. For example, 2 and 4 are consecutive even numbers and 1 and 3 are consecutive odd numbers. The SSAT is not going to ask you if numbers are consecutive, but they will ask you to apply this information. If you see the words "consecutive even numbers" or "consecutive odd numbers", circle them because it is really easy to do just plain consecutive numbers and forget about the even or odd.

- Consecutive just means in a row
- Look out for consecutive even and consecutive odd numbers because it is easy to forget the even or odd part

On the SSAT, they don't directly test these definitions. They are not going to ask you which of the following numbers is positive. But they will ask you to apply the information.

Interpreting Equation/Inequality Language

On the SSAT, you may see language that describes in words what you often see written as an equation or inequality.

You just have to translate these words into an equation or inequality in order to solve.

Here is a cheat sheet for some of what you may see:

If they say:	Then it can be written as:
X is between 3 and 5	$3 < X < 5$
X is greater than 6	$X > 6$
X is less than 10	$X < 10$

The thing that you need to keep in mind about between, greater than, and less than is that they don't include the numbers themselves. For example, if X is between 3 and 5, then it cannot be either 3 or 5.

Here is an example of how these concepts are tested:

1. M is a whole number that is between 5 and 8. M is also between 6 and 13. Which of the following is M?
   (A) 5
   (B) 6
   (C) 7
   (D) 7.5
   (E) 8

If we drew out a number line, we would see that our number has to be bigger than 6 and smaller than 8. Because the problem uses the word between we know that 6 or 8 cannot be included. That leaves us with choices C and D. However, the problem also says that M is a whole number. The number 7.5 is not a whole number, so choice D is out. Choice C is correct.

There will also be times when the wording gives hint as to what operation should be completed.

Here is a guide to some of the language you may see:

If the test says:	You should:
…of…	Multiply
…how many more…	Find the difference (subtract)
…how many times…	Divide
…sum…	Add
…difference…	Subtract
…divisible by…	Divide and look for a number that does not leave a remainder
…into how many…	divide

Once again, the test usually asks you to apply this information.

Here are some examples of how this information is tested:

2. On Wednesday, Sheila had sold 324 boxes of cookies. Her goal was to sell 410 boxes by Sunday. How many more boxes of cookies must she sell between Wednesday and Sunday?
   (A) 34
   (B) 76
   (C) 86
   (D) 410
   (E) 734

The question uses the words how many more, so we know we need to subtract, or find the difference.

If we do $410 - 324$, then we get 86, so choice C is correct.

Here is another example of a question that tests your ability to apply equation language:

3. Ben brought 3 dozen donut holes to share with his classmates. If he wants to evenly divide them among the nine students in his class, and there will be none left over, then how many donut holes does each student get?
   (A) 1
   (B) 2
   (C) 3
   (D) 4
   (E) 5

There are a total of 36 donut holes (a dozen means 12, so 3 dozen is 3 × 12, which is equal to 36). There are 9 kids in the class, so we divide 36 by 9 and get that each student gets 4 donut holes. Choice D is correct.

Sometimes they give us a question where the division problem does not come out evenly. Then we have to decide whether to round up or to round down.

Here is an example:

4. Julie has 75 cents. She wants to buy lollipops that are 14 cents each. How many lollipops can she buy?
   (A) 4
   (B) 5
   (C) 6
   (D) 7
   (E) 8

To solve this problem, we have to see how many 14's we can get from 75. If we divide 75 by 14, we get 5 with a remainder of 5. Since Julie can only buy a lollipop when she has the full 14 cents, she can only buy five lollipops. Choice B is correct.

Here is another one to try: (Remember to think about whether to round up or round down!)

5. Grace needs to buy 23 t-shirts for her class. The t-shirts come in packages of 10. How many packages must she buy?
   (A) 1
   (B) 2
   (C) 3
   (D) 4
   (E) 5

The trick to this problem is that Grace has to buy more t-shirts than she needs. If we divide 23 by 10, then we get 2 with remainder 3. However, we can't not have enough t-shirts, so with this problem type, the remainder tells us to round up. The correct answer is C.

The Math Facts You Need to Know

Don't worry, you don't need to learn a lot of math facts for this test.

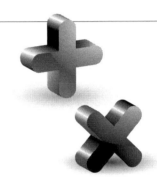

It is helpful to know:
1. Multiplication/Division facts up to 12
2. Single digit addition/subtraction facts
3. Multiples of 15 (15, 30, 45, 60, 75, 90)
4. Multiples of 25 (25, 50, 75, 100, and so on)

We won't take the time to go over these facts here, but if you are rusty on your facts, be sure to practice them. There are a ton of good apps out there and it doesn't really matter which one you choose. You just want to make sure that these facts are automatic for you since no calculators are allowed on the SSAT.

It can also be helpful to know some basic divisibility rules. You don't absolutely have to know these as long as you can do the problems out by hand. It can save you time if you know divisibility rules, however.

Here are some of the easier rules. There are rules for numbers divisible by 7 and 8, but they are really hard to remember and therefore not so helpful!

If …	Then it is divisible by…
the number is even	2
you add up all the digits of the number and the result is divisible by 3 (ex: 231 = 2 + 3 + 1 = 6 and 6 is divisible by 3)	3
the last two digits of your number are divisible by 4 (ex: 549624 and 24 is divisible by 4)	4
the number ends in 0 or 5	5
the number is divisible by both 2 and 3	6
you add up all the digits and the result is divisible by 9 (ex: 3726 = 3 + 7 + 2 + 6 = 18 and 18 is divisible by 9)	9
the number ends in 0	10

Here is a basic example of how divisibility could be tested:

6. Which of the following answer choices is divisible by 6?

(A) 824
(B) 826
(C) 828
(D) 866
(E) 904

If a number is divisible by 6, it must be divisible by both 2 and 3. All of the answer choices are even, so they are all divisible by 2. Now, to see if the numbers are divisible by 3 we have to add up the digits and see if that number is divisible by 3.

(A) $8 + 2 + 4 = 14$- not divisible by 3

(B) $8 + 2 + 6 = 16$ - not divisible by 3

(C) $8 + 2 + 8 = 18$- IS divisible by 3

(D) $8 + 6 + 6 = 20$- not divisible by 3

(E) $9 + 0 + 4 = 13$- not divisible by 3

Since only answer choice C is divisible by both 3 and 2, it is the only answer choice that is divisible by 6. Answer choice C is correct.

Some other questions don't use the word "divisible" at all! But they are still testing divisibility.

Here is an example:

7.   If $t/4$ is a whole number, which of the following could be t?
(A) 748
(B) 758
(C) 774
(D) 802
(E) 814

In order for $t/4$ to be a whole number, t would have to be evenly divisible by 4. To figure out if a number is evenly divisible by 4, we look just at the last two digits. If we look at answer choice A, the last two digits are 48. 48 is divisible by 4, so choice A is correct.

Other problems set up a situation where items must be divided evenly. In these problems, look for the answer choice that is divisible by the number of people that the item will be distributed among.

Here is an example:

8. Tommy brought a cake to school for his birthday. There are 12 kids in his class. If he wants every student to get an equal number of pieces of cake, and there will be none left over, into how many pieces could he cut his cake?
   (A) 6
   (B) 18
   (C) 20
   (D) 36
   (E) 40

This question uses the words "into how many", so we know that we have to divide. It also tells us that he wants each student to have the same number of pieces of cake, so we are looking for a number that is divisible by 12, since there are twelve students. The only answer choice that is evenly divisible by 12 is choice D, so it is correct.

Finally, we have a doozy of a problem. It uses the word average, but it isn't really an average problem. Since an average is equal to $\frac{sum}{\#\ of\ things}$, if the average is to be a whole number, then the sum must be evenly divisible by the number of things.

Also, you should know that if a number is divisible by another number, then it is also divisible by its factors. This is actually what our rule for being divisible by 6 is based on. Two and three are both factors of six, so if a number is divisible by both two and three, then the number will be divisible by six. This is particularly helpful when you are dealing with bigger numbers than we have rules for. For example, let's say a question asks us if something is divisible by 15. Three times five is fifteen, so if the number was divisible by BOTH three and five, it would be divisible by fifteen.

The following problem is very challenging- don't even worry about doing it if you are in fifth grade. None of the other fifth graders will be able to do this problem, either, so your percentile score would not be lowered for not doing this problem.

Here is a challenging problem:

9.   Maria wanted to know what the average class size was at her school. She took the total enrollment at her school and divided it by the number of classes. She found that the average class size was exactly 18 students. Which of the following could NOT have been the total number of students at her school?
(A) 1080
(B) 1140
(C) 1134
(D) 1152
(E) 1170

In order to solve this problem, we need to find the answer choice that is NOT evenly divisible by 18. If we divide 18 into factors, we can see that nine times two gives us eighteen. That means that if answer choice is divisible by both two and nine, then it is divisible by 18.   All of the answer choices are even, so we can't rule any out for not being divisible by 2. So we need to look for the answer choice that is NOT divisible by nine since it is a NOT question. If we add up the digits of answer choice B, we get 6, which is not divisible by nine and therefore 1140 is not divisible by nine.

Choice B is correct.

Operations you need to know

You will also need to know how to do the basic operations. You will need to add, subtract, multiply (including multi-digit numbers), and divide (including long division). We aren't going to work on that here, but if your skills are rusty, be sure to do a little practice.

The trick to SSAT questions that test math facts and basic operations is that you often have to figure out exactly what they are testing. The SSAT is much more about application than just listing facts.

Operations

You know that the basic mathematical operations are addition, subtraction, multiplication, and division. On the SSAT they will not ask you to add 2 numbers or to do a long division problem! That is too easy. Instead they will "hide" these basic operations in problems that look hard but are really easy if you practice.

Here is an example.

10. If $35 + 35 + 35 + 35 + 35 = 5 \times \blacksquare$, then what number goes in the $\blacksquare$?
    (A) 5
    (B) 30
    (C) 35
    (D) 55
    (E) 175

The left side of the equation is an addition problem, and the right side is asking you to turn it into a multiplication problem. When we add 35 to itself 5 times, then that is the same thing as multiplying 35 by 5, so the multiplication problem will be 5×35. The correct answer is C.

Now try this one.

11. If $10 + 126 + \Delta + \odot = 221$ then $\Delta + \odot =$
    (A) 10
    (B) 85
    (C) 126
    (D) 306
    (E) Cannot be determined

In order to solve this problem, we must first add together the numbers given on the left side of the equation. This gives us $136 + \Delta + \odot = 221$. If we then subtract the 136 from both sides, we get that $\Delta + \odot$ must be equal to 85, so choice B is correct.

Another problem type asks you to apply what you know about carrying numbers when you add.

Remember that when you add 2 numbers together, you have to carry a 1 to the next place if the sum of any column is greater than 10. Look at this example.

$$\begin{array}{r} 3724 \\ + 1198 \\ \hline 4922 \end{array}$$

In the first column to the right, we add 4 and 8 and get 12. We write down the 2 then carry the 1 to the next column over. We add $2 + 9 + 1$ (this is the one that we carried over), and get 12 again. So we write down the two and carry the one to the next column to the left. We add 7+1+1 (this is the one that we carried over) and get nine. Since nine is not a two digit number, we don't have to carry over anything to the last column on the left.

Now try this problem.

12. What are the possible values for ▲ in the problem below?

```
   3724
+  11▲8
   49□2
```

(A) 0, 1, or 2
(B) 2, 3, or 4
(C) 5, 6, or 7
(D) 6, 7, or 8
(E) 7, 8, or 9

Let's look at each column. We added the 4 + 8 and got 12, so we wrote down the two and carried the one to the next column. Now we will add 2 + 1 + ▲ to get □. We can't figure this out, not yet. But go to the next column on the left and notice that, since 7 + 1 doesn't add up to 9, we must have carried a 1 from the previous added column. So now we know that 2 + 1 + ▲ has to be greater than or equal to 10. This happens only if ▲ is 7, 8, or 9. Any of these values would work. Answer choice E is correct.

Now try this problem:

13. 738
   + 11▲6   The value for ▲ could be which of the following digits?
     19□4

(A) 0
(B) 1
(C) 3
(D) 5
(E) 6

The easiest way to solve this problem is to go through the process of adding. If we add the first column on the right, we get a total of 14 and carry the one to the next place. That gives us a total of 4 plus the triangle in the next column. If we look at the next column to the left, we can see that a one must have been carried from the previous column. Since that column adds to 4 as is, we can see that the missing digit must be atleast 6 in order for us to have to carry a one. Answer choice E is correct.

Similar problems exist for multiplication and division. Let's review these basic operations.

When you do a division problem, such as $6\overline{)43}$ the work is: $6\overline{)43}$ with 7 above, 42 below, and 1 remainder.

Remember that you can say that the quotient (7) times the divisor (6) plus the remainder (1) is equal to the original number that was being divided.

- $quotient \times divisor + remainder = number\ that\ was\ divided$

Now try this problem:

14. Chloe divides a number by 6 and gets 4 with a remainder of 3 as her answer. What was the original number?
    (A) 20
    (B) 21
    (C) 24
    (D) 27
    (E) 28

In order to solve this problem, we first have to multiply the divisor (6) times the quotient (4). This gives us 24. Then we add in the remainder (3) and get that the original number must have been 27. Answer choice D is correct.

15. For the division problem $8\overline{)\odot}$, if the answer is between 6 and 7, then a possible value for $\odot$ is
    (A) 24
    (B) 32
    (C) 36
    (D) 48
    (E) 54

If the answer to $8\overline{)\odot}$ were 6, then the problem would look like this: $8\overline{)\odot}$ with 6 above. In this case, the value for $\odot$ would be 48 if we multiply the quotient (answer) by the divisor. If the answer to $8\overline{)\odot}$ were 7, then the problem would look like this: $8\overline{)\odot}$ with 7 above and the value of $\odot$ would be 56. The problem states that the answer is between 6 and 7, and so the value of $\odot$ is between 48 and 56. Thus, the correct answer choice is E.

Another type of problem that tests your understanding of operations uses multiplication. Consider this problem:

```
  12
×43
  36
 48
516
```

Another way to write this problem would be (12 × 3) + (12 × 40). This is where the values of 36 and 48 come from in the work shown just above the answer. But look again at the 48. It is NOT really 48. It is really 480, because it is the answer to (12 × 40) which is 480. There should really be a 0 after the 48, but we use a quick version to shorten the problem, and so we don't write the 0. In school, you probably learned to put in your own zero to mark the place value. On the SSAT, this is what they are really testing with this problem type.

Use this information to answer the following question.

16. What is the value of the digit 7 in the line with the arrow?

```
 137
 ×24
 548
 274  ⬅
```

(A) 7
(B) 70
(C) 700
(D) 7,000
(E) 70,000

If you remember the hint from the discussion above, you know that 274 is really 2,740. Thus, the value 7 is really 700. The correct answer is C.

Now try this one:

17.

$$137$$
$$\underline{\times 24}$$
$$548 \Longleftarrow$$
$$\underline{274}$$

What is the value of the 5 in the line with the arrow?
(A) 5
(B) 50
(C) 500
(D) 5,000
(E) 50,000

In this case, the number 548 is in the first line of the multiplication problem, so it isn't too tricky. There is no missing digit, so the answer is C.

Squaring and Square Roots

Squaring a number means to multiply it by itself. For example, if square 6, then we write it as $6^2 = 6 \times 6 = 36$. To square an expression like *(x + 2)*, we write it as *(x + 2)²*. Another way to write the same expression would be *(x + 2)(x + 2)*.

Taking a square root of a number is going backwards from squaring. To find the square root of 36, we ask ourselves, "What number times itself is equal to 36?" The answer is 6.

We use a special symbol for a square root. To take the square root of 36, we write it in symbols as $\sqrt{36}$. Here is another square root: $\sqrt{64} = 8$.

On the SSAT it is helpful just to know a few perfect squares:

$$1^2 = 1$$
$$2^2 = 4$$
$$3^2 = 9$$
$$4^2 = 16$$
$$5^2 = 25$$
$$6^2 = 36$$
$$7^2 = 49$$

$8^2 = 64$

$9^2 = 81$

$10^2 = 100$

Here is how this concept is tested on the SSAT:

18. If a number multiplied by itself is 400, what is the number?
    (A) 2
    (B) 10
    (C) 20
    (D) 40
    (E) 100

The question is a restatement of the definition of squaring a number. It really is asking what number squared is equal to 400? The easiest way to solve this is to try each answer choice.

(A) 2	$2^2 = 2 \times 2 = 4$	No
(B) 10	$10^2 = 10 \times 10 = 100$	No
(C) 20	$20^2 = 20 \times 20 = 400$	Yes
(D) 40		
(E) 100		

The correct answer is C.

Here is another one to try:

19. If $\#x\# = x^2$, then what is $\#4\#$ equal to?
    (A) 4
    (B) 8
    (C) 16
    (D) 20
    (E) 24

The trick to solving this problem is to not get thrown off by the # signs. You aren't supposed to know what they mean- they are made up. The question is telling us what we should do with them. If x is surrounded by # signs, then we are supposed to square x. Since 4 is also surrounded by # signs, then we have to square four in order to find the answer. Since 4 squared is 16, answer choice C is correct.

20. The expression $\sqrt{49}(2x+5)$ is equal to

(A) $5 + 14x$

(B) $35 + 2x$

(C) $35 + 14x$

(D) $40 + 16x$

(E) 49

To solve this problem, we first have to take the square root of 49. Since *7 × 7 = 49*, the square root of 49 is 7. We now have *7(2x + 5)*, so we have to use the distributive power. We are left with *14x + 35*. If we look at our answer choices however, *14x + 35* is not one of them. We are using addition, though, so we can use the commutative power to rearrange the equation and get *35 + 14x*. Answer choice C is correct.

Place Value— Just the Important Stuff

Another basic concept that is tested is place value.

Consider the number 354. This number is really made up of 3 separate numbers: The "4" is 4 ones. The "5" is 5 tens, and the "3" is 3 hundreds. These 3 numbers are added up as 4 + 50 + 300 to get 354. Here is a chart to help you remember place values.

We will use the number 457,208.196 as an example.

4	5	7	2	0	8	.	1	9	6
Hundred thousands	Ten thousands	Thousands	Hundreds	Tens	Ones	Decimal point	Tenths	Hundredths	Thousandths

Look at the digit 2, which is in the hundreds place. It represents a value of 200, because it represents 2 hundreds which is 200. Similarly, the digit 5 represents 5 ten thousands, so its value is 50,000.

For another example, think of the number 829. The number 829 is really the result of adding three numbers together: 8 hundreds (800) plus 2 tens (20) plus 9 ones (9).

Another way to think of the number 829 is: $(8 \times 100) + (2 \times 10) + (9 \times 1)$.

Let's do a sample problem:

462.3<u>4</u>1

21. In the above number, what is the value of the underlined digit?
    (A) 4 hundredths
    (B) 4 tenths
    (C) 4 ones
    (D) 4 tens
    (E) 4 hundreds

In the above question, the underlined digit is in the hundredths place. That means that the value of the 4 is 4 hundredths, so answer choice A is correct. The trick with these types of questions is to pay close attention to whether or not the answer choice has the "th" at the end of it.

Here is another place value problem that may look a little different from how you have seen place value tested before.

22. In the number 537.981, which digit has the GREATEST value?
    (A) 3
    (B) 5
    (C) 7
    (D) 8
    (E) 9

This question is a little tricky. Be careful not to just choose the greatest number. 9 may be the biggest number, but in the context of the whole number, the nine is only worth $9/10$. The digit 5 is actually worth 500 in the number given, so that digit has the greatest value. Choice B is correct.

Here is another question that uses place value:

23. 8■,649

   In the number given above, the thousands digit has been replaced with a black box. If the number above is less than 86,649, then what is the largest digit that could replace the black box?

   (A) 1
   (B) 2
   (C) 6
   (D) 5
   (E) 7

If the total number is less than 86,649, then we know that the missing thousands digit must be less than 6. Answer choice D is correct.

The next problem uses place value, but it is pretty challenging! If you are in fifth grade, don't even worry about trying to do it- other students your age won't be able to do it, so your percentile score will not be affected if you skip this question.

24. Which fraction is equal to the decimal $\boxdot$ .4?

   (A) $\dfrac{10 \times (\boxdot + 4)}{10}$

   (B) $\dfrac{(10 \times \boxdot) + 4}{10}$

   (C) $\dfrac{\boxdot + 3}{10}$

   (D) $\dfrac{\boxdot + 3}{100}$

   (E) $\dfrac{(10 \times \boxdot) + 4}{100}$

The easiest way to solve this problem is to fill in our own number for $\boxdot$. Let's make $\boxdot$ equal to 2. That means that $\boxdot$.4 would be equal to 2.4. Now we can plug in 2 for $\boxdot$ in the answer choices and see which answer choice gives us 2.4.

   (A) $\dfrac{10 \times (\boxdot + 4)}{10} = \dfrac{10 \times (2+4)}{10} = \dfrac{60}{10} = 6$

   (B) $\dfrac{(10 \times \boxdot) + 4}{10} = \dfrac{(10 \times 2) + 4}{10} = \dfrac{24}{10} = 2.4$

   (C) $\dfrac{\boxdot + 3}{10} = \dfrac{2+3}{10} = \dfrac{5}{10} = 0.5$

(D) $\dfrac{\square+3}{100} = \dfrac{2+3}{100} = \dfrac{5}{100} = 0.05$

(E) $\dfrac{(10 \times \square)+4}{100} = \dfrac{(10 \times 2)+4}{100} = \dfrac{24}{100} = 0.24$

From this, we can see that only choice B gives us 2.4 when we plug in 2 for the $\square$ symbol. Answer choice B is correct.

Now you have the fundamentals that you need to do well on the math section of the SSAT. Be sure to complete the math fundamentals practice set to reinforce your learning. Remember, the most important part of the practice set is figuring out WHY you missed the questions that you answer incorrectly.

Math Fundamentals Practice Set

1. Kim plans to buy balloons for a party. She wants one balloon for the back of each chair and there a total of 27 chairs at the party. If the balloons come in packages of six, how many packages of balloons must she buy?
   (A) 4
   (B) 5
   (C) 6
   (D) 8
   (E) 9

2. In the number 253.$\underline{8}$74, what is the value of the underlined digit?
   (A) 8 hundredths
   (B) 8 tenths
   (C) 8 oneths
   (D) 8 ones
   (E) 8 tens

3. John can't remember the number of home runs that Daniel made last season. Daniel writes on paper: $16 < x < 20$ and $x > 18$. If x is the number of home runs that Daniel made, what is the value of x?
   (A) 16
   (B) 17
   (C) 18
   (D) 19
   (E) 20

4. Let k be an even number. What is the next consecutive even number?
   (A) $k - 2$
   (B) $k + 1$
   (C) $k + 2$
   (D) $2k + 1$
   (E) $2k + 2$

5. The square of a number is 4 more than the square root of 25. What is the number?
   (A) 3
   (B) 4
   (C) 5
   (D) 8
   (E) 9

6. What is the value of the digit 6 in the line with the arrow pointing to it?

276
×12
552
276 ⟵

(A) .6
(B) 6
(C) 60
(D) 600
(E) 6,000

7. At Lora's grandmother's 90th birthday party, there are 5 identical cakes. A total of 60 people are at the party. Into how many pieces should each cake be cut, to make sure that each person gets at least 1 piece of cake?

(A) 6
(B) 7
(C) 8
(D) 9
(E) 12

8. If the division problem $\Delta \overline{)e}^{\,W}$ has a remainder of 1, then what is an expression for e?

(A) e × W − 1
(B) Δ × W + 1
(C) e × Δ + 1
(D) Δ + W × 1
(E) W × Δ − 1

9. What is the digit represented by ◹ in the following addition problem?

6 2 3
+9◹Δ
15 7 1

(A) 0
(B) 1
(C) 2
(D) 3
(E) 4

10. If $\boxed{x} = x^2 - 7$ then $\boxed{4} =$
    (A) 6
    (B) 7
    (C) 8
    (D) 9
    (E) 10

11. If $\frac{x}{3}$ is a whole number, which of the following could be x?
    (A) 236
    (B) 359
    (C) 451
    (D) 502
    (E) 654

12. Which of the following numbers is divisible by 9?
    (A) 234
    (B) 256
    (C) 302
    (D) 436
    (E) 469

13. If $26 + 26 + 26 + 2\ 6 = 4 \times \blacksquare$, then what number should replace $\blacksquare$?
    (A) 3
    (B) 4
    (C) 26
    (D) 52
    (E) 104

14. If $11 + 85 + o + \Delta = 159$, then $o + \Delta =$
    (A) 51
    (B) 63
    (C) 96
    (D) 104
    (E) 159

15. The expression $\sqrt{36}(3x + 2) - 3$ is equal to

    (A) $\sqrt{33} + 3x + 2$

    (B) $6x + 6$

    (C) $12x - 3$

    (D) $18x + 9$

    (E) $18x - 6$

Challenge problems- do not worry if you cannot get these problems- remember that schools are looking at your percentile score!

16. Which fraction is equal to the decimal $\odot.3$?

    (A) $\dfrac{10 \times (\odot + 3)}{10}$

    (B) $\dfrac{(10 \times \odot) + 3}{10}$

    (C) $\dfrac{\odot + 3}{10}$

    (D) $\dfrac{\odot + 3}{100}$

    (E) $\dfrac{(10 \times \odot) + 3}{100}$

17. Karl wanted to know the average class size at his school. He took the total number of students at his school and then divided by the number of classes. He found that the average class size was exactly 15 students. Which of the following could have been the total number of students at his school?

    (A) 650

    (B) 725

    (C) 805

    (D) 845

    (E) 855

Answers for Math Fundamentals Practice Set

1. B
2. B
3. D
4. C
5. A
6. C
7. E
8. B
9. E
10. D
11. E
12. A
13. C
14. B
15. D
16. B
17. E

Patterns

On the SSAT, you will generally find a few questions that require you to recognize and use patterns.

In the section, we will work on how to do the following:

- Identify patterns
- Use a pattern to predict what a particular element in the pattern will be

Patterns are all around us. You might notice that in the lunch line that first in line is a girl, then a boy, then a girl, then a boy. If this pattern kept up, you would guess that a girl would be next in line. It's as simple as this with patterns, only the examples change a bit, and sometimes there are numbers or objects rather than people.

Let's go back to the lunch line. What if you had to find out if the 50th person in line was a girl or a boy? Now it doesn't look so easy! One way to do this would be to get paper and write the gender of every one of the people in line, like this: Girl, Boy, Girl, Boy, Girl, Boy, Girl, Boy, … all the way to the 50th person and you could then say, "The 50th person in line is a boy!" But that is too much work, when there is a really easy way to figure this out without all that work.

Notice that the girls are first, third, fifth, seventh, and so on. And boys are second, fourth, sixth, eighth, and so on. Do you see a pattern emerging? Girls are all the odd-numbered people in line, and boys are all the even-numbered people in line! So the 50th person in line (an even number) will definitely be a boy. And the 27th person in line would be… (now it is easy!) a girl.

This example is pretty easy because we only have to deal with odd or even numbers to get the answer. Sometimes the pattern will not be so obvious, but with practice it can be just as easy.

Here is an example.

1. Pam is making kabobs, where you put meat and vegetables on a skewer. She always puts the meat and vegetables on the skewer in the same order: beef, onion, green pepper, and tomato. The skewer is very long, so Pam will repeat this pattern many times. What is the 18th item that Pam will put on the skewer?
   (A) Beef
   (B) Onion
   (C) Green Pepper
   (D) Tomato
   (E) Cannot be determined

Let's make a chart to help with seeing the pattern, counting the order below each choice:

Beef	Onion	Green Pepper	Tomato
1	2	3	4
5	6	7	8
9	10	11	12
13	14	15	16
17	18	19	20

We see that onion will be the 18th item chosen to go on the skewer. The correct answer is B.

There is an easier way to do this problem than count over and over, which takes a lot of time. Notice that the counting for the tomato column is an old friend: it is a list of multiples of 4. So if you were asked to find a really big number, like the 39th item to go on the kabob, it would be really easy. From the times table for 4s, if you extended it, it would be easy to see that the 40th item is tomato, because 40 is a multiple of 4. The 39th item would be 1 less than tomato, which would be green pepper.

Now you try this one:

2. You are sorting coins and putting them in a pattern of penny, nickel, dime, and repeating this over and over. What is the 37th coin that you would put in the pattern?
(A) Penny
(B) Nickel
(C) Dime
(D) Quarter
(E) Cannot be determined

To solve this problem, notice that there are 3 elements in our pattern before it repeats. If there were 36 coins, then there would be exactly 12 of the patterns. This means that the pattern starts over with the 37th coin. Since a penny is the first item in our pattern, that would be the 37th coin. Choice A is correct.

The two problems above were about repeating patterns and how to solve them. Let's now look at how patterns can go on forever and not repeat. We can still solve them pretty easily.

Look at this pattern of numbers: $1, 4, 7, 10, \ldots$ What would be the next number in the pattern? If you said 13, you are correct. This pattern is called an arithmetic sequence, and is very easy to spot. Each time, you add 3 to the previous number to get the next number, and that is why 13 is the next number in the sequence.

Sometimes there will be 2 patterns in the numbers if the numbers are fractions.

Here is an example of how this could be tested on the SSAT:

3. What is the next number in this set of fractions? $\frac{1}{5}, \frac{2}{6}, \frac{3}{7},$

(A) $\frac{1}{8}$

(B) $\frac{2}{8}$

(C) $\frac{3}{4}$

(D) $\frac{4}{8}$

(E) $\frac{5}{6}$

Look at the numerators (top numbers). Their pattern is to increase by 1 each time. The next numerator would be 4. Now look at the denominators (bottom numbers). They also get bigger by 1 each time, so the next denominator would be 8. Thus, the answer would be $\frac{4}{8}$, or answer choice D.

Here is another one for you to try:

4. Given the pattern $\frac{1}{4}$, $\frac{2}{8}$, $\frac{3}{12}$, $\frac{4}{\odot}$, then what is the value for $\odot$?
   (A) 1
   (B) 8
   (C) 14
   (D) 16
   (E) 20

If we look closely at the pattern, we can see that with each fraction, the top number has one added to it. But the bottom number has four added to it each time. If we add 4 to 12, we get 16, so choice D is correct.

Here is a tougher question about number patterns, where you don't see the pattern, but instead you have to follow the directions to make the pattern yourself.

5. A number is 3 more than twice the previous number. The first number in the pattern is one. What is the 3rd number in the pattern?
   (A) 3
   (B) 5
   (C) 7
   (D) 10
   (E) 13

You start with the number 1. The directions say to take twice the number 1 and then add 3 to it. Twice the number 1 is 2, and then when you add 3 to it, you get 5. So 5 is the second number in the pattern. Now repeat the directions to find the next number, but start with the number 5. Take twice 5 and add 3. This gives *10 + 3*, which is 13, so answer choice E is correct.

Here is an example for you to try:

6. Here is a pattern of numbers: 1, 1, 2, 3, 5, 8, … To get the third number, add the first and second numbers. To get the fourth number, add the second and third numbers. To get the fifth number, add the third and fourth numbers. If we continue this pattern, then what is the seventh number in the pattern?
   (A) 9
   (B) 12
   (C) 13
   (D) 16
   (E) 20

This one isn't so bad, even though it looks kind of scary. You just have to follow the instructions that they give for creating the pattern. To get the seventh number, you simply add together the fifth and sixth number, or do 5 + 8. Answer choice C is correct.

Now you know how to ace pattern problems on the SSAT! Be sure to complete the patterns practice set.

Patterns Practice Set

1. The teacher is collecting photos of all the 6th graders' pets. She ends up with 20 dog photos, 20 cat photos, 20 hamster photos and 20 snake photos. She puts them on a big display board, always putting a dog, then a cat, then a snake, then a hamster photo, and then she starts over with the same pattern. What is the 54th photo that she will put on the display board?
   (A) Dog
   (B) Cat
   (C) Snake
   (D) Hamster
   (E) Cannot be determined

2. A number is said to be a square number if that number of objects can be arranged in rows such that a square can be built from the number of objects. Here is a diagram for the first three square numbers:

   1 •   4   9

   What are the next 2 square numbers?
   (A) 10 and 12
   (B) 12 and 16
   (C) 16 and 20
   (D) 16 and 25
   (E) 25 and 36

3. Find the value of ∇ in this pattern. $\frac{1}{5}, \frac{4}{5}, \frac{7}{5}, \frac{10}{5}, \frac{\nabla}{5}$
   (A) 11
   (B) 12
   (C) 13
   (D) 15
   (E) 17

4. Here is a pattern: $\frac{2}{5}, \frac{3}{6}, \frac{4}{7}, \frac{5}{8}, \ldots \frac{13}{\square}$. If this pattern is continued, what is the value of $\lozenge$?

   (A) 16
   (B) 18
   (C) 20
   (D) 24
   (E) 30

5. Janice is stringing colored popcorn on a long string. She always puts white, then green, then red, in that order. Which piece of popcorn could not be green?

   (A) the 5th piece
   (B) the 14th piece
   (C) the 21st piece
   (D) the 29th piece
   (E) the 65th piece

Answers to Patterns Practice Set

   1. B
   2. D
   3. C
   4. A
   5. C

Fractions and Decimals

Fractions and decimals on the SSAT really are not too bad. The problems tend to be pretty predictable problem types. Remember to pay attention to what makes each problem type unique as you work through this section.

On the SSAT, you will need to be able to:

- Use a picture to determine what fraction is shaded
- Add, subtract, multiply, and divide fractions
- Figure out another amount when we are given a fractional part
- Compare fractions
- Convert mixed numbers and improper fractions
- Know what a ratio is and how it can function like an equivalent fraction
- Multiply decimals

Use a picture to determine what fraction is shaded

The first type of fraction problem that we will go over is how to tell what fraction of a picture is shaded.

The basic strategy for these problem types is that you need to divide your picture into pieces.

- Divide your pictures into pieces

This is easy if it is a figure that can be divided into equally sized pieces.

For example, if we have the following picture:

 In this picture, we can see that there are four equally sized pieces. Two of those four pieces are shaded, so $1/2$ of the figure is shaded

Here is an example of how this could be tested on the SSAT:

1. In the hexagon in Figure 1, what fraction of the hexagon is shaded?
   (A) $1/2$
   (B) $1/3$
   (C) $1/4$
   (D) $1/5$
   (E) $1/6$

In order to solve this problem, draw in lines that divide the hexagon into equal pieces.

It should look like this:

Now we can clearly see that one part out of six is shaded in, so the correct answer is choice E.

Sometimes you will have to divide a figure into unequal pieces to see what works. This question type always asks you to identify which figures have one-half shaded in. It would be possible to write this question without using $1/2$ as the fraction that is shaded, but that would be a much harder problem type so the SSAT uses $1/2$.

Here is an example of a figure that has one-half shaded in but isn't easily divisible into pieces that are all the same size.

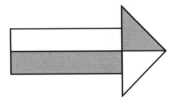

The key to these questions are just to match up parts that would be the same and then make sure that half of those parts are shaded.

Here is one for you to try:

2. Which of the following figures is NOT shaded in one-half of its region?

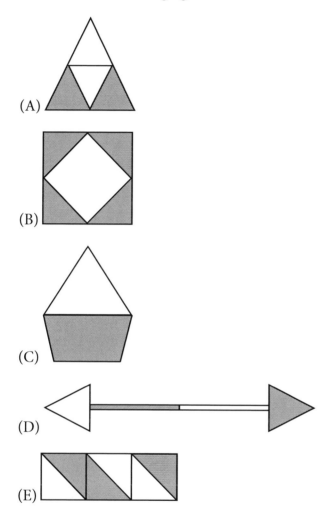

(A)

(B)

(C)

(D)

(E)

To answer this question, simply match up the shaded regions to identical non-shaded regions. If that doesn't work, then you have your correct answer. Choice C is the correct answer.

Add, Subtract, Multiply, and Divide Fractions

There are some basic rules that you need to know for fractions on the SSAT. They won't be tested directly, but you will need them in order to solve other questions correctly.

They are:

1. You can multiply or divide the numerator (top number) as long as you multiply or divide the denominator (bottom number) by the SAME number. This allows us to create *equivalent fractions*- or fractions that are equal in value.

2. If you want to add or subtract fractions, you have to get the same bottom number (or common denominator). Use equivalent fractions to do that. You then add or subtract the top numbers, but keep the same bottom number (common denominator).

3. If you want to multiply fractions, you multiply across the top and then across the bottom (you DON'T figure out a common denominator).

4. If you want to divide fractions, you flip the second fraction and then multiply.

Creating equivalent fractions:

The cardinal rule for equivalent fractions is that if you multiply the top by some number, you must also multiply the bottom by the same number in order for the value to remain the same. This works when you multiply or divide the top and bottom by the same number. You can NOT add or subtract the same number from both the top and the bottom and keep the same value, however.

For example:

$$\frac{1}{2} \times \frac{2}{2} = \frac{2}{4}$$ Since we multiplied the numerator (top number) and denominator (bottom number) by the same number, we know that $\frac{1}{2} = \frac{2}{4}$

$$\frac{1+2}{2+2} = \frac{3}{4}$$ Since we added the same number to the numerator and denominator, $\frac{1}{2}$ is NOT equal to $\frac{3}{4}$

To add or subtract fractions:

We use equivalent fractions to get the same bottom number, otherwise known as a common denominator.

We then add (or subtract) across the top and keep the common denominator as the denominator in our answer.

For example:

Let's say our problem looks like this:

$$\frac{1}{2} + \frac{2}{3} = ?$$

We are looking for a number that both denominators go into, or are factors of. 2 and 3 both go into 6, so 6 will be our common denominator.

$$\frac{1}{2} \times \frac{3}{3} = \frac{3}{6}$$

$$\frac{2}{3} \times \frac{2}{2} = \frac{4}{6}$$ We use equivalent fractions to get a common denominator

We can now add the equivalent fractions:

$$\frac{3}{6} + \frac{4}{6} = \frac{7}{6}$$ We add across the top but keep the common denominator

We aren't quite done yet. We now have a fraction where the top number is bigger than the bottom number (an improper fraction). To fix this, we can break apart the fraction.

$$\frac{7}{6} = \frac{6}{6} + \frac{1}{6}$$ We break the fraction apart so that we can see how many "ones" we have and what fraction is left.

Finally, we can create a mixed number as an answer.

$$\frac{6}{6} + \frac{1}{6} = 1 + \frac{1}{6} = 1\frac{1}{6}$$

To multiply fractions:

We can simply multiply across the top and across the bottom.

For example:

$$\frac{1}{2} \times \frac{2}{3} = \frac{2}{6}$$

We then have to reduce the fraction since there is a number that goes into both the numerator and denominator. We use our rule of equivalent fractions (do the same to the top and bottom), only this time we are dividing.

$$\frac{2 \div 2}{6 \div 2} = \frac{1}{3}$$

Our final answer would be $\frac{1}{3}$.

Those really are the basics for what you need to know about fractions. That's not so bad, right?

Now let's move on to how these basics will be tested.

Dividing fractions:

To divide fractions, we just flip the second fraction and multiply.

For example, let's say our problem was:

$$^2/_3 \div ^4/_5$$

In order to find our answer, we flip the second fraction and multiply, so our problem becomes:

$$\frac{2}{3} \times \frac{5}{4} = \frac{2 \times 5}{3 \times 4} = \frac{10}{12}$$

We aren't quite done yet, we still have to reduce. Since 10 and 12 are both divisible by 2, we divide the top and the bottom by 2.

$$\frac{10 \div 2}{12 \div 2} = \frac{5}{6}$$

Our final answer is $^5/_6$.

One other thing to keep in mind is order of operations, or PEMDAS

PEMDAS tells us that we do whatever is in parentheses first.

Here is how one of these questions could look on the SSAT:

3. $7 \times (^1/_3 + ^2/_3)$
   (A) $^7/_6$
   (B) $^{14}/_3$
   (C) $^{14}/_6$
   (D) $^{14}/_9$
   (E) 7

To solve this problem, we first have to do what is in parentheses. If we add $1/3 + 2/3$, then we get 1. We didn't even have to find a common denominator! Our new problem is now 7×1, so the answer is just 7, or choice E.

Here is another one for you to try:

4. $15 \left(6/9 - 2/3\right) =$
   (A) 0
   (B) 1
   (C) 3
   (D) 5
   (E) 15

To solve this problem, first we have to get a common denominator to do what is in parentheses. The denominators (9 and 3) are both factors of 9, so we make that our common denominator. We can leave the first fraction alone, but we have to use equivalent fractions to get a denominator of 9 on the second fraction.

$$\frac{2 \times 3}{3 \times 3} = \frac{6}{9}$$

Now that we have equivalent fractions, we can see that our problem in parentheses is really:

$$\frac{6}{9} - \frac{6}{9} = 0$$

This tells us that our main problem is really 15×0, and since anything times zero is zero, the correct answer is choice A.

The way that the SSAT tests division of fractions is pretty straight-forward.

Here is how fraction division looks on the SSAT:

5. $\frac{1}{5} \div \frac{1}{5} =$

   (A) 0
   (B) $\frac{1}{10}$
   (C) $\frac{2}{10}$
   (D) 1
   (E) 10

In order to solve this problem, we just flip the second fraction and multiply. It would look like this:

$$\frac{1}{5} \div \frac{1}{5} = \frac{1}{5} \times \frac{5}{1} = \frac{5}{5} = 1$$

Choice D is correct.

Other problems ask you to perform multiple operations.

Here is an example:

6. Sarah has the following problem:
   $$\frac{1}{3} \; \Delta \; \frac{1}{5}$$

   She should replace the Δ with which of the following operations if she wants the result to be as small as possible?

   (A) ÷
   (B) ×
   (C) +
   (D) −
   (E) the result would be the same for each of the operations

In order to answer this question, we have to do each of the operations.

We can just make a list:

(A) $1/3 \div 1/5 = 1/3 \times 5/1 = 5/3$

(B) $1/3 \times 1/5 = 1/15$

(C) $1/3 + 1/5 = 5/15 + 3/15 = 8/15$

(D) $1/3 - 1/5 = 5/15 - 3/15 = 2/15$

(E) the result would be the same for each of the operations- this answer choice is definitely out since we can see that the answers are not the same for each operation

We can clearly see that multiplying gives us the smallest number, so choice B is correct.

Figuring out another amount when we are given a fractional part

The next problem type will tell you what a fraction of something is equal to then ask you to find another amount. For example, they might tell you that $2/7$ of a jug holds 3 cups and then ask you how much liquid there would be if the jug was $4/7$ full.

The trick to these questions is not to find the full amount and then try to convert back into the desired fraction. Instead think about what the first fraction must be multiplied by in order to get the second fraction.

- Think about what you have to multiply the first fraction by in order to get the second fraction

Here is what this type of question could look like on the SSAT:

7. If $3/7$ of a number is 60, then what is $6/7$ of that same number?
   (A) 180
   (B) 120
   (C) 90
   (D) 30
   (E) 15

To solve this problem, just think about what you have to multiply $3/7$ by in order to get $6/7$. We would have to multiply by 2. So we multiply 60 by 2 and get 120, or answer choice B.

Here is another one to try that requires you to convert from one fraction to another:

8. If $1/3$ of a can of soda contains 12 grams of sugar, then how many grams of sugar are there in the full can of soda?
    (A) 4
    (B) 6
    (C) 12
    (D) 24
    (E) 36

In order to solve this problem, think about what you would have to multiply $1/3$ by in order to get a whole. We have to multiply $1/3$ by 3 in order to get one. Since we multiplied the fraction by 3, we also multiply the grams of sugar by 3 to get 36. Choice E is correct.

Harder still is when we have to break apart a fraction to get the missing piece.

Here is an example:

9. Charles poured 4 cups into a pitcher and found that it was $2/3$ full. How many cups does the pitcher hold when it is full?
    (A) 2
    (B) 3
    (C) 4
    (D) 6
    (E) 8

For this problem, we have to figure out what fraction needs to be added to make the pitcher full. Since it is $2/3$ full now, another $1/3$ would need to be added. $1/3$ is half of $2/3$, so 2 cups would equal $1/3$ of the pitcher. If we add 2 cups to the 4 cups that were already in the pitcher, it would be full, so the whole pitcher holds 6 cups. Answer choice D is correct.

Here is another one for you to try:

10. A bottle that is $\frac{3}{4}$ full contains 15 cups of juice. If the bottle was full, how many cups of juice would it hold?
    (A) 10
    (B) 12
    (C) 15
    (D) 18
    (E) 20

In order to solve this problem, we have to think about what fraction of the bottle needs to be added in order to make it full. Since it is $\frac{3}{4}$ full, we would need to add $\frac{1}{4}$ of the bottle in order to make it full. If three parts out of 4 is equal to 15, we divide 15 by 3 to get that one part out of 4, or $\frac{1}{4}$ would be equal to 5. We need to add 5 cups of juice in order to fill the pitcher. That means that the whole pitcher could hold 20 cups and answer choice E is correct.

Comparing fractions

Some questions will ask you to compare fractions on the SSAT.

In order to do this, you need to get a common denominator. Rather than looking for a denominator that all of the answer choices go into, I recommend setting up a different equivalent fraction for each answer choice. These equivalent fractions should have the same denominator as the answer choice so that they can be easily compared.

- Set up an equivalent fraction for each answer choice

Take a look at this example:

11. Which of the following fractions is less than $1/4$?
    (A) $10/40$
    (B) $4/8$
    (C) $5/16$
    (D) $3/20$
    (E) $7/24$

To solve, I just make a chart:

Answer choice	Equal to $1/4$	Which is smaller?
(A) $10/40$	$10/40$	Equal
(B) $4/8$	$2/8$	$1/4$
(C) $5/16$	$4/16$	$1/4$
(D) $3/20$	$5/20$	Answer choice!
(E) $7/24$	$6/24$	$1/4$

From my chart, I can see that only choice D is smaller than $1/4$, so choice D is correct.

Here is another one for you to try:

12. Which of the following fractions is greater than $\frac{2}{3}$?
    (A) $\frac{8}{12}$
    (B) $\frac{7}{14}$
    (C) $\frac{7}{9}$
    (D) $\frac{11}{18}$
    (E) $\frac{1}{6}$

Again, let's create our chart!

Answer choice	Equal to $\frac{2}{3}$	Which is greater?
(A) $\frac{8}{12}$	$\frac{8}{12}$	Equal
(B) $\frac{7}{14}$	14 isn't divisible by 3, so equivalent fractions won't work. But I can see that $\frac{7}{14}$ is equal to one half, so I know it has to be less than $\frac{2}{3}$	$\frac{2}{3}$
(C) $\frac{7}{9}$	$\frac{6}{9}$	Answer choice!
(D) $\frac{11}{18}$	$\frac{12}{18}$	$\frac{2}{3}$
(E) $\frac{1}{6}$	$\frac{4}{6}$	$\frac{2}{3}$

We can see that answer choice C is correct.

Converting mixed numbers and improper fractions

The next thing that you will need to know how to do is to convert between mixed numbers and improper fractions.

A mixed number is simply a number that has a whole number part and a fraction part. Here is an example:

$$3\,{}^{1}/_{5}$$

An improper fraction is just a fraction where the top number (numerator) is bigger than the bottom number (denominator).

The easiest way to convert from a mixed number to an improper fraction is to break the mixed number down into ones and then convert those ones into fractions.

Here is how it would look with our above example:

$$3\,{}^{1}/_{5} = 1 + 1 + 1 + \frac{1}{5} = \frac{5}{5} + \frac{5}{5} + \frac{5}{5} + \frac{1}{5} = \frac{16}{5}$$

This tells us that $3\,{}^{1}/_{5} = \frac{16}{5}$.

On the SSAT, they don't just come out and ask you to convert between the two, however.

Here is what a question might look like that tests this skill:

13. How many sixths are there in $3\,{}^{1}/_{6}$?
    (A) 1
    (B) 6
    (C) 12
    (D) 18
    (E) 19

To figure out how many total sixths we have in that mixed number, we must rewrite the number in terms of sixths. This means converting it into an improper fraction.

It would look like this:

$$3\,\tfrac{1}{6} = 1 + 1 + 1 + \frac{1}{6} = \frac{6}{6} + \frac{6}{6} + \frac{6}{6} + \frac{1}{6} = \frac{19}{6}$$

This tells us that there are 19 sixths in $3\tfrac{1}{6}$ so answer choice E is correct.

Here is another one for you to try:

14. How many fourths are there in $2\,\tfrac{3}{4}$?
    (A) 12
    (B) 11
    (C) 8
    (D) 3
    (E) 2

First, let's convert that mixed number into an improper fraction:

$$2\,\tfrac{3}{4} = 1 + 1 + \frac{3}{4} = \frac{4}{4} + \frac{4}{4} + \frac{3}{4} = \frac{11}{4}$$

This tells us that there are 11 fourths in $2\,\tfrac{3}{4}$, so answer choice B is correct.

Ratios— what they are and how they can function like equivalent fractions

A fraction compares a part to the whole. For example, if I have four pieces of paper and one is red and three are green, then I would say that $\tfrac{1}{4}$ of my paper is red.

- Fractions compare a part to the whole

A ratio, on the hand, compares part to parts. For example, in our above example, the ratio of red to green paper is 1 to 3.

- Ratios compare part to part

In a lot of ways, we can treat ratios like fractions. If we multiply or divide one part of the ratio by a number, then as long as we multiply or divide the other part of the ratio by the same number then the ratios are equivalent.

For example, the ratio of 1 to 3 is equal to the ratio of 3 to 9 since we multiplied both numbers by 3. Just like with equivalent fractions, it doesn't work if we add or subtract the same number.

- We can create equivalent ratios just like we create equivalent fractions

Here is an example of how this could be tested on the SSAT:

15. The ratio of 5 to 9 is equal to the ratio of
    (A) 25 to 81
    (B) 15 to 27
    (C) 10 to 27
    (D) 18 to 10
    (E) 9 to 5

Let's look at the answer choices. To get answer choice A, you would have had to square each number, which means you are not multiplying by the same number so choice A is out. In choice B, you would have to multiply 5 by 3 to get 15. You would also have to multiply 9 by 3 to get 27. Since you are multiplying by the same number in both cases, answer choice B is correct.

Here is another question:

16. The ratio of red candies to blue candies is 2 to 3. If there are 8 red candies, how many blue candies are there?
    (A) 24
    (B) 18
    (C) 16
    (D) 12
    (E) 6

In order to solve, we need figure out what 2 had to be multiplied by in order to get 8. We had to multiply 2 by 4 to get 8, so we also have to multiply 3 by 4. That tells us that there would be 12 blue candies so choice D is correct.

Here is another example that is a little trickier:

17. Figure 2 shows a rectangular swimming pool. The shaded area is the deep end and the unshaded area is the shallow part. A rope separates the two sections. If the distance from one wall to the rope in the shallow end is 6 m (as shown) and the distance from one wall to the rope in the deep end is 18 m (as shown), then what is the ratio of the shallow end to the deep end?

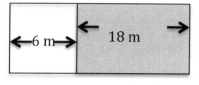

Figure 2

(A) $^6/_{24}$

(B) $^1/_3$

(C) $^3/_1$

(D) $^3/_{18}$

(E) $^3/_4$

To solve this problem, we have to keep in mind that a ratio is part to part and NOT part to whole. Since the shallow end is 6m and the deep end is 18m, the ratio of the shallow end to the deep end would be $^6/_{18}$. This is not an answer choice, however. But remember that just like fractions, ratios can be reduced. We can divide both the numerator and denominator by 6. This leaves us with $^1/_3$, or answer choice B.

Multiplying decimals

Decimal multiplication is pretty straightforward if you remember one rule:

- If you move the decimal point to the *right* when you begin the problem, you will move it to the *left* when you get the answer.

Here are the steps for multiplying decimals:

1. If any of the numbers in your question have decimal points, move the decimal point to the right. Keep track of how many decimal places you moved in total!
2. Multiply these numbers together.
3. Take the answer that you get and then move the decimal place back to the left the same number of spaces that you moved it to the right before multiplying.

Here is an example:

$34 \times 0.03 =$

Step 1: Move the decimal place to the right- and keep track of the number of spaces moved.

34×3 We moved the decimal place on the second number two spots to the right- we need to remember that

Now we can just use multiplication with whole numbers.

$34 \times 3 = 102$ In the first step, we moved the decimal two places to the *right*, so now we move it two places to the *left* in the final answer

Our next step is to move the decimal back two spaces to the left to get our final answer.

$34 \times 0.03 = 1.02$

Here is how this concept is tested on the SSAT:

18. If pencils cost $0.15 each at the school store, how much would it cost to by 8 pencils?
    (A) $0.75
    (B) $1.05
    (C) $1.20
    (D) $1.25
    (E) $1.35

To solve this problem, we have to move the decimal to two places to the right. This allows us to do 15×8 as our multiplication problem. We get 120 as our answer. Now we have to move the decimal back two places to the left. That gives us 1.20 as our final answer, so choice C is correct.

Here is another one for you to try:

19. At a store, each bouncy ball costs $0.69. About how much would it cost to buy 3 bouncy balls at this store?
    (A) $2.50
    (B) $2.10
    (C) $2.00
    (D) $1.80
    (E) $1.40

Did you see that the question said "about how much"? These words about tells us to round. So we can round the $0.69 to $0.70. If our problem is now 0.70 × 3, we would move the decimal one place to the right so that we can do 7 × 3, which gives us an answer of 21. To get our final answer, we have to move the decimal back one place to the left. This leaves us with 2.1, or choice B.

Now you know how to do well on fraction and decimal problems on the SSAT! Be sure to complete the fraction practice set to reinforce your learning.

Fractions and Decimals Practice Set

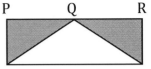

Figure 1

1. Figure 1 shows a rectangle. If Q is the midpoint of side PR then what fraction of the rectangle is shaded?
   (A) $^1/_6$
   (B) $^1/_5$
   (C) $^1/_4$
   (D) $^1/_3$
   (E) $^1/_2$

2. $^2/_5 \div {^2/_5} =$
   (A) 0
   (B) $^4/_{10}$
   (C) $^4/_5$
   (D) 1
   (E) 4

3. $16 \left(^6/_9 - {^2/_3} \right) =$
   (A) 0
   (B) $^1/_{16}$
   (C) 1
   (D) 15
   (E) 16

4. If $^3/_7$ of a number is equal to 15, then what is $^6/_7$ of that same number equal to?
   (A) 45
   (B) 30
   (C) 15
   (D) 7.5
   (E) 5

5. A jar contains 2 cups of sauce. If it is currently $^2/_3$ full, then how many cups can the jar hold when it is completely full?
   (A) 1
   (B) 2
   (C) 3
   (D) 5
   (E) 6

6. If a type of pudding has 200 calories in a $^1/_3$ cup serving, then how many calories are there in 1-cup serving?
   (A) 100
   (B) 150
   (C) 200
   (D) 400
   (E) 600

7. Which of the following is less than $^2/_3$?
   (A) $^6/_9$
   (B) $^{11}/_{15}$
   (C) $^8/_{16}$
   (D) $^{13}/_{18}$
   (E) $^{15}/_{21}$

8. How many fifths are there in $4\,^2/_5$?
   (A) 22
   (B) 20
   (C) 5
   (D) 4
   (E) 2

9. If each eraser costs $0.19, then about how much would it cost to by 9 erasers?
   (A) $1.50
   (B) $1.80
   (C) $1.85
   (D) $1.90
   (E) $2.10

10. The ratio of 3 to 4 is the equivalent to the ratio of
   (A) 6 to 9
   (B) 6 to 16
   (C) 9 to 16
   (D) 9 to 18
   (E) 12 to 16

Answers for Fraction and Decimals Practice Set

1. E
2. D
3. A
4. B
5. C
6. E
7. C
8. A
9. B
10. E

Percent Problems

Percent problems are really just glorified fraction and decimal problems.

On the Middle Level SSAT you will have to:

1. Find a percent
2. Given a certain percentage of a number, find a different percentage of the same number

Keep in mind that per means "out of" and cent means "hundred".

Therefore, percent means out of a hundred.

How To Find a Percent of a Number

The easiest way to solve percent problems is to use equivalent fractions and cross-multiplying.

Here is the basic setup:

$$\frac{part}{whole} = \frac{percent}{100}$$

For example, let's say that we wanted to find 20% of 50.

First, we set up the equivalent fraction and plug in what we have been given.

$$\frac{x}{50} = \frac{20}{100}$$

Now we use the principles of equivalent fractions to solve. To get from 50 to 100, we have to multiply by 2. So what number do we have to multiply by 2 in order to get 20? We have to multiply 10 by 2 in order to get 20, so $x = 10$ and 20% of 50 is 10.

Here is a question for you to try:

1. If there are 25 students in a class, but only 15 of them are in the school band, then what percent of the students are in the school band?
   (A) 4%
   (B) 25%
   (C) 50%
   (D) 60%
   (E) 75%

In order to solve this problem, we just have to set up a basic equivalent fraction problem:

$$\frac{15}{25} = \frac{x}{100}$$

To get from 25 to 100, we have to multiply the denominator by 4. That means that we also have to multiply the numerator by 4. 15 times 4 is 60, so answer choice D is correct.

Here is another problem to try:

2. There are ten fish in an aquarium. If three of the fish are green, what percent of the fish are NOT green?
   (A) 30 %
   (B) 40%
   (C) 50%
   (D) 60%
   (E) 70%

The only trick to this question is that the test writers tell you how many fish are green but then ask for the percent of fish that are NOT green. If three fish are green, then seven fish are not green. We can set up a basic equivalent fraction:

$$\frac{7}{10} = \frac{x}{100}$$

To get from 10 to 100, we had to multiply the denominator by 10. That means we also have to multiply the numerator by 10, so we get that 70% of the fish were not green. Answer choice E is correct.

Here is yet another problem to try:

3. If there are 50 students on a bus and they are all in the fifth grade, what percent of students on the bus are fifth graders?
   (A) 5%
   (B) 25%
   (C) 50%
   (D) 100%
   (E) 110%

This is kind of a tricky question. We don't actually have to do any calculating! If all of the students on the bus are in fifth grade, then 100% of the students on the bus are fifth graders. Answer choice D is correct.

If you are given a certain percent of a number, how to find a different percentage of the same number

This problem type should look very familiar to you. It is just like the problem type we covered in the fractions section where they give you one fraction of a number and ask for another fraction of the same number. There is a reason they are so similar- a percentage is just another way to write a fraction!

- These problems are just like the questions that give you one fraction of a number and ask for a different fraction

We will use the same basic technique. Rather than solving for the original number, we will just figure out what they multiplied the original percent by to get the new percent.

- Don't find the original number

Here is an example:

4. If 20% of a number is 15, then what is 40% of the same number?
   (A) 3
   (B) 6
   (C) 15
   (D) 30
   (E) 60

To answer this question, let's think about how we get from 20% to 40%. We multiply by 2, right? So that means we can just multiply 15 by 2 to get 40% of the same number. The correct answer is choice D.

Here is another one for you to try:

5. If 30% of a number is 25, then what is 90% of the same number?
   (A) 75
   (B) 50
   (C) 25
   (D) 10
   (E) 5

Let's think about how we get from 30% to 90%. We multiply by 3. That means that we can just multiply 25 by 3 to get what 90% of that same number would be. Choice A is correct.

Now you know what you need in order to ace percent problems! Be sure to complete the percent practice set.

Percent Practice Set

1. If 25% of a number is 16, then what is 50% of the same number?
   (A) 4
   (B) 8
   (C) 16
   (D) 24
   (E) 32

2. There are ten players on the tennis team. Four of these players only play doubles and the rest of the players only play singles. What percent of the players only play singles?
   (A) 100%
   (B) 60%
   (C) 50%
   (D) 40%
   (E) 10%

3. If all 30 kids in a class have returned their permission slips, what percent of the class has returned their permission slips?
   (A) 0%
   (B) 3%
   (C) 30%
   (D) 60%
   (E) 100%

4. If 15% of a certain number is 30, then 30% of the same number is
   (A) 7.5
   (B) 15
   (C) 30
   (D) 60
   (E) 90

5. In a class of 25 students, none of the students did their homework. What percent of the students did their homework?
   (A) 0%
   (B) 20%
   (C) 25%
   (D) 50%
   (E) 100%

Answers to Percent Practice Set

1. E
2. B
3. E
4. D
5. A

Average Problems

Average problems on the SSAT aren't so bad because they fall into very predictable categories.

The types of problems you will see include:

1. Questions that use the basic definition of an average
2. Consecutive number average problems
3. Weighted averages
4. Questions that don't even use the word average… but we can use the concepts of averages to solve

Average problems on the SSAT use the following equation:

$$\frac{sum\ of\ numbers}{number\ of\ numbers} = average$$

Sometimes you will have to manipulate the equation to get:

$$sum\ of\ numbers = number\ of\ numbers \times average$$

Questions that use the basic definition of an average

In general, to find an average of numbers, we add together the numbers and then divide by the number of numbers.

For example:

Let's say we are given the numbers 4, 8, and 12 and need to find an average.

Here is what the math would look like to find the average:

$$\frac{4 + 8 + 12}{3} = \frac{24}{3} = 8$$

On the SSAT, they are not likely to ask you just to find the average of three numbers, however!

They add a whole bunch of other words so that not every student will answer these questions correctly. Just follow carefully and look out for words like NOT.

- Follow average questions closely and look out for details that could trip you up

Here is what these average questions could look like on the actual SSAT:

1. Jean is thinking of two numbers whose average is equal to half of the average of 10 and 22. Which of the following could be the two numbers that Jean is thinking of?
   (A) 2 and 20
   (B) 4 and 18
   (C) 5 and 11
   (D) 9 and 11
   (E) 15 and 17

The trick to this question is that it is a multi-step problem and we have to not stop before we are done. First, we have to find the average of 10 and 22. The math would look like this:

$$\frac{10 + 22}{2} = \frac{32}{2} = 16$$

Now we know that the average of 10 and 22 is 16. We can't stop here and find an answer choice whose average is 16, however. We need to find an answer choice where the average of the two numbers is half of 16, or 8.

Now let's find the averages for those answer choices:

(A) $\frac{2+20}{2} = \frac{22}{2} = 11$

(B) $\frac{4+18}{2} = \frac{22}{2} = 11$

(C) $\frac{5+11}{2} = \frac{16}{2} = 8$

(D) $\frac{9+11}{2} = \frac{20}{2} = 10$

(E) $\frac{15+17}{2} = \frac{32}{2} = 16$

We can see that only answer choice C gives us an average of 8, so that is our correct answer. We can also see that 5 and 11 are respectively each half of 10 and 22. It makes sense then that the average of 5 and 11 would be half the average of 10 and 22.

Here is another one for you to try:

2. Of the following pairs of numbers, which pair does NOT have an average equal to one-third the average of 9 and 21?
    (A) 4 and 6
    (B) 3 and 7
    (C) 1 and 9
    (D) 14 and 16
    (E) 2 and 8

To answer this question, we first need to find the average of 9 and 21. The math would look like this:

$$\frac{9 + 21}{2} = \frac{30}{2} = 15$$

Now, we have to remember to take one-third of that average. One-third of 15 is 5, so we are looking for an answer choice that gives us an average that is NOT 5. The only answer choice that does not give us average of 5 is choice D. This is the correct answer. Answer choice D gives us an average of 15, not 5.

Consecutive number average problems

Sometimes they will give you an average for consecutive whole numbers, consecutive odd numbers, or consecutive even numbers.

You should rejoice when you see these problems- as long as you know the problem type, consecutive number average problems are super easy.

The only potential trick is forgetting what kind of numbers they are using (consecutive, consecutive even, or consecutive odd) or forgetting whether they are asking for the smallest number or the greatest number. Circle what kind of numbers they are looking for and what they are asking for and you will be just fine.

- Circle what kind of numbers are being used (consecutive, consecutive even, or consecutive odd)
- Circle what they are asking for (smallest or greatest number)

Here is an example of how a question could look on the SSAT:

3. The average of three consecutive odd numbers is 11. What is the smallest number?
    (A) 9
    (B) 10
    (C) 11
    (D) 12
    (E) 13

First of all, did you remember to circle "consecutive odd" and "smallest number?" Good. Consecutive number problems are pretty easy -- the average is just the middle number. The strategy for this is just to draw a blank for each number. Insert the average in the middle blank and find what they are looking for.

For the above example:

1. Draw a blank for each number: ____ ____ ____

2. Insert the average in the middle: ____ 11 ____

3. Find what they are looking for: 9   11 ____

Since the smallest number is 9, answer choice A is correct.

Here is another one for you to try:

4. If the average of five consecutive whole numbers is 12, what is the largest one?
    (A) 7
    (B) 10
    (C) 12
    (D) 14
    (E) 17

For this problem, we draw out five slots and then put twelve in the middle. We then fill in the other slots like so:

_____ _____ 12   13   14

From this, it is clear to see that 14 is the largest number, so answer choice D is correct.

Weighted average problems

Sometimes you have to find a total average given the average of a couple of groups. What you need to do is use the following equation to find the sum of each group:

$$sum\ of\ group = number\ of\ numbers \times average$$

Then use the average equation again to find the total average.

$$\frac{sum\ of\ group\ 1 + sum\ of\ group\ 2}{total\ number\ of\ numbers} = overall\ average$$

This is called a weighted average. You don't need to remember this term -- you just need to know NOT to add the two averages together and divide by 2.

Here is an example of how this is tested on the SSAT:

5. The average length of four kittens is 20 inches. The average length of a different set of two kittens is 14 inches. What is the average length of all six kittens?
   (A) 14
   (B) 15
   (C) 16
   (D) 18
   (E) 20

To solve this problem, we first have to figure out the sum of all the lengths. If we multiply 4 times 20, we get that the sum of the lengths of the kittens that are 20 inches long is 80 inches. Then, to find the sum of the kittens that are 14 inches long, we multiply 2 times 14 to get 28. Now we add 80 and 28. This tells us that the sum of the lengths of all the kittens in 108. If we divide that sum by the total number of kittens (6), we get that the average length is 18 inches, or choice D.

Sometimes we have to do even more steps. Some problems require us to change some of the numbers and find a new average.

Here is how this looks on the SSAT:

5. The average price of three dolls is $18. The price is reduced by $3 for two of these dolls. What is the new average price for these three dolls?
    (A) $18
    (B) $17
    (C) $16
    (D) $15
    (E) $14

We can treat this as a weighted average problem. We now have one doll that is $18 and two dolls that are $15. We have to find the sum of their prices. There are two dolls that cost $15, so the sum of the prices for those two dolls is $30. Then we add in the doll that remained $18. This tells us that altogether the three dolls cost $48. We divide $48 by 3, since there are three dolls, and find that the new average price is $16. Answer choice C is correct.

Those were tricky, so let's try another one:

6. At the beginning of the year, the average weight of four students was 48 kilograms. By the end of the year, two students had each gained 4 kilograms and the other two students had not gained or lost any weight. What was the average of the four students weights at the end of the year (in kilograms)?
    (A) 48
    (B) 49
    (C) 50
    (D) 51
    (E) 52

In this problem, we can just say that each student weighed 48 pounds to begin with. This may not be accurate, but what matters is that the sum of their weights gives us 48 pounds as an average. At the end of the year, we now have two students who weigh 48 kg and two students who weigh 52 kg. We need to do a weighted average. Here is what the math looks like:

$$\frac{sum\ of\ group\ 1 + sum\ of\ group\ 2}{4} = \frac{(2 \times 48) + (2 \times 52)}{4} = \frac{96 + 104}{4} = \frac{200}{4} = 50$$

This tells us that the new average weight of the group is 50 kg. Choice C is correct.

Questions that don't even use the word average... but we can use the concepts of average to solve

You may see problems that use the word "sum" that allow us to use the concepts of average.

Let's take a look at the following problem:

8. The sum of five consecutive numbers is 105. What is the largest number?
   (A) 19
   (B) 20
   (C) 21
   (D) 22
   (E) 23

We can use what we learned from consecutive number average problems. When the numbers are consecutive, the middle number will also be the average. To find the average (and the middle number) we have to do the following:

$$average = \frac{sum}{number\ of\ numbers} = \frac{105}{5} = 21$$

Now we can draw out five slots (since we have five numbers), and put the average in the middle:

_____ _____ __21__ _____ _____

From here, we just fill in consecutive numbers to get:

__19__ __20__ __21__ __22__ __23__

We can see that 23 is the largest number so choice E is correct.

Here is another one for you to try:

9. If the sum of three consecutive odd numbers is 45, then what is the smallest number?
   (A) 11
   (B) 13
   (C) 14
   (D) 15
   (E) 17

Since it is a consecutive number problem, we know that the middle number is also the average. To find the average, we divide the sum by 3, since that is the number of numbers. That tells us that the average, as well as the middle number, is 15. Now, did you remember that they wanted consecutive odd numbers? That means that our numbers must be 13, 15, and 17. Now we just have to keep it straight that they are asking for the smallest number, so choice B is correct.

Another type of problem doesn't require you to use average, but it does require you to use sum. It is also not that different from the problems that we did earlier where some members of a group increased in size or weight, but others did not. So we will cover them here- even if they aren't strictly average problems.

Here is an example:

10. If the sum of the ages of four children is 18, what will be the sum of their ages three years from now?
    (A) 32
    (B) 30
    (C) 26
    (D) 24
    (E) 22

The trick to this question is that we can't just add four years to 18 and be done with it. Each child will be three years older, and there are 4 children, so the sum of their ages will actually increase by 12. The correct answer is B.

Here is another one for you to try:

11. The sum of the weights of three children is 118 pounds. If two of those children gain 4 pounds each and the third child's weight remains the same, then what is the sum of their new weights? (in pounds)
    (A) 118
    (B) 122
    (C) 124
    (D) 125
    (E) 126

For this problem, we have to keep in mind that there were 2 children who each gained 4 pounds. This means that the overall sum would increase by 8, not just 4. That means we have to add 8 to 118 in order to get 126, or answer choice E.

Another type of problem that doesn't use the word "average" but we can use the average principles for is problems with rate.

These problems are some of the most difficult, so if these problems seem really hard, don't spend too much time on them. Particularly if you are in 5th, or even 6th, grade.

Keep in mind that when they give a rate in terms of miles per hour, what that gives us is the average distance travelled in a one hour block.

Let's take a look at how this could be tested on the SSAT:

12. Kim competed in triathlon. First, she swam a mile at the rate of 2 miles per hour. Then, she ran 12 miles at the rate of 6 miles per hour. Then she rode 20 miles on her bike at the rate of 30 miles per hour. How long did it take her to complete the entire triathlon?
    (A) 34 minutes
    (B) 1 hour 30 minutes
    (C) 2 hour 52 minutes
    (DA) 3 hours
    (E) 3 hours 10 minutes

This problem is a doozy, so let's break it down into pieces. In the first segment of the race, she swam a mile. Since her rate was two miles per hour, it would have taken her half an hour to swim one mile, or 30 minutes. In the next segment, she ran 12 miles. Since her speed was 6 miles per hour, it would have taken her two hours, or 120 minutes, to complete the running segment. Then she rode her bike for 20 miles. Since she was going at the rate of 30 miles per hour, we have to use a proportion to solve. Since 20 miles is $2/3$ of 30 miles, it would have taken her $2/3$ of an hour, or 40 minutes. If we add all the minutes together, we get $30 + 120 + 40 = 190$. Now the trick is that we have to convert this back into hours and minutes. Since $190 = 60 + 60 + 60 + 10$, we know that 190 minutes equals 3 hours and 10 minutes. Choice E is correct.

Keep in mind that this is a VERY challenging question. If you get it right, that's great. But you will be among the few that do! Schools are looking at your percentile scores, so if you felt that this question was way over your head, it probably won't affect your percentile score.

Average Problem Practice Set

1. If the average of five consecutive even numbers is 22, what is the smallest one?
    (A) 17
    (B) 18
    (C) 20
    (D) 22
    (E) 27

2. If the sum of three consecutive even numbers is 60, then what is the smallest of these numbers?
    (A) 18
    (B) 19
    (C) 20
    (D) 21
    (E) 22

3. The average height for three students was 46 inches. If two of the students each grew 3 inches and the third student's height did not change, then what is their new average height?
    (A) 50
    (B) 49
    (C) 48
    (D) 47
    (E) 46

4. Of the following pairs of numbers, which pair has an average that is twice the average of 6 and 14?
    (A) 5 and 15
    (B) 4 and 16
    (C) 18 and 21
    (D) 3 and 5
    (E) 12 and 28

5. Lucy is thinking of two numbers whose average is half the average of 5 and 11. Which of the following pairs could NOT be the numbers that Lucy is thinking of?

(A) 1 and 7

(B) 2 and 6

(C) 3 and 5

(D) 7 and 8

(E) 4 and 4

6. When three children added their ages together, they got 19 as the sum. What will be the sum of their ages four years from now?

(A) 60

(B) 55

(C) 40

(D) 31

(E) 24

Challenge problem:

7. Julian and Tommy ran in a 6-mile race. Julian ran the first 4 miles at 10 miles per hour. He then walked the rest of the race at 4 miles per hour. Tommy jogged the first 3 miles at 6 miles per hour. He then walked the rest of the race at 3 miles per hour. Who won the race and by how many minutes did he win?

(A) The two boys finished at the same time

(B) Tommy won by 36 minutes

(C) Tommy won by 12 minutes

(D) Julian won by 12 minutes

(E) Julian won by 36 minutes

Answers to Average Practice Set

1. B
2. A
3. C
4. E
5. D
6. D
7. E

Solving Equations

On the SSAT Middle Level, solving equations will be tested in several ways. The problem types include:

- Basic solving for a variable
- Solving for a variable and then using that value to find another number
- Setting up equations and solving for overlapping groups
- Creating and using inequalities

Basic solving for a variable

The basic goal of solving equations is to get a variable by itself –or to isolate it.

There are two basic rules for isolating a variable:

1. Use PEMDAS (order of operations), but in reverse
2. Do the opposite operation in each step

What does this mean to reverse the order of PEMDAS?

Here is a basic example:

$x + 2 = 4$

(In each step, notice that we do the *opposite* operation in order to simplify the equation.)

$x + 2 = 4$ The left side has *addition*, so we must *subtract*.
$-2 \quad -2$
$x = 2$ The problem is solved, the value of x is 2.

Here is another example:

$$\frac{1}{2}x = 7$$ The left side has *division* by 2 so we must *multiply* by 2.

$$\times 2 \quad \times 2$$
$$x = 14$$ The problem is solved. The value of x is 14.

Here is an example of how this problem could look on the SSAT:

1. If $Q + 7 = 7$, the Q is equal to
   (A) 0
   (B) $\frac{1}{7}$
   (C) 1
   (D) 7
   (E) 14

In this question, we want to get Q by itself. Currently, Q has a 7 added to it. To get rid of that 7, we have to do the opposite, or subtract 7 from both sides. That leaves us with $Q = 0$, so answer choice A is correct.

Here is another one for you to try:

2. If $12N = 12$, then $N =$
   (A) 0
   (B) $\frac{1}{12}$
   (C) 1
   (D) 6
   (E) 12

In order to solve, we have to get N by itself. Right now N is multiplied by 12, so we have to do the opposite, and divide both sides by 12. If we do that, we get $N = 1$, so answer choice C is correct.

Sometimes they get a little trickier. As long as you stick to reverse PEMDAS and do the opposite to isolate a variable, you will be just fine.

Here is an example:

3. If $8 \times R + 2 = 5$, then $R =$
   (A) ⅜
   (B) ⅝
   (C) 2
   (D) 8
   (E) 16

To solve, first we have to see if there is anything added or subtracted. There is a 2 added to the side with the variable, so we subtract that from both sides and get $8 \times R = 3$. Now we have an 8 that is multiplied by the variable, so we divide both sides by 8 and get $R = ⅜$, so answer choice A is correct.

Solving for a variable and then using that value to find another number

These questions ask you to solve for a variable and then use that value to solve another problem.

These aren't hard, you just have to remember to complete all the steps. It is very easy to solve for the variable and then choose that as your answer choice. To get around that, be sure to circle what they are asking for.

- Circle what the question is asking for

Here is what these questions look like on the SSAT:

4. If $T + 8 = 8$, then $T + 16 =$
   (A) 0
   (B) 1
   (C) 4
   (D) 8
   (E) 16

If $T + 8 = 8$, then T must equal zero. If we plug in zero for T in the second equation, then we get $0 + 16 = 16$, so choice E is correct.

Here is another one for you to try:

5. If $300 + h = 600$, then $500 + h =$
    (A) 300
    (B) 400
    (C) 600
    (D) 800
    (E) 1000

To solve the first equation, we have to subtract 300 from both sides in order to get h by itself. This gives us $h = 300$. We aren't done yet, though! The question asks us for then $500 + h$, so we have to plug in 300 for h and solve. We get $500 + 300 = 800$, so answer choice D is correct.

Sometimes these problems also mix operations.

Here is an example:

6. If $5 \times T = 35$, what does $5 + T$ equal?
    (A) 0
    (B) 1/7
    (C) 1
    (D) 7
    (E) 12

First we have to solve for T. If we divide both sides of the first equation by 5, then we get $T = 7$. The question asks for $5 + T$, however, so we have to keep going. If we substitute in 7 for T, we get $5 + 7 = 12$, so answer choice E is correct.

Setting up equations and solving for overlapping groups

Another type of problem that you will see is where they give the values for overlapping line segments.

To solve these problems:

- Mark all the information given on the drawing
- Set up equations so that you can see how all the parts are related

Here is what these questions look like on the test:

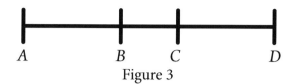

Figure 3

7. In figure 3 above, the distance between B and D is 12. The distance between A and C is also 12. If the distance between C and D is 8, what is the distance between A and B?
    (A) 6
    (B) 7
    (C) 8
    (D) 10
    (E) 12

To solve this equation, the first step is to mark information given. Our picture now looks something like this:

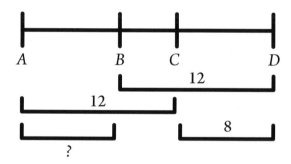

This allows us to set up some equations and solve.

We can see that:

$BC + CD = 12$

Since we know that $CD = 8$, we can solve to get that $BC = 4$.

We can also see that:

$AB + BC = 12$

Since we now know that $BC = 4$, we can solve to get $AB = 8$.

Since they were asking for the length of AB, we know that answer choice C is correct.

Here is another one for you to try:

(It might look scary, but it is really just the same type of problem)

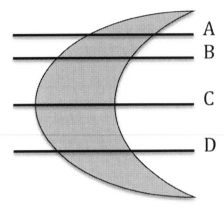

Figure 4

4. In Figure 4, the shaded region is divided by lines A, B, C, and D. The shaded area between lines A and C is 25 square yards. The area of the shaded region between lines B and D is 30 square yards. If the area of the shaded region between lines C and D is 15, then what is the area, in square yards, of the shaded region between A and B?
    (A) 10
    (B) 15
    (C) 20
    (D) 25
    (E) 35

First, mark the distances on your picture. From that, you can see that:

$$AC = AB + BC = 25$$

We can also see that:

$$BC + CD = BD$$

Since we are given that the area between C and D is 15 and that the area between B and D is 30, it is not hard to figure out that the area between B and C is also 15.

Now we can plug this back into our first equation and solve:

$$AB + BC = 25$$
$$AB + 15 = 25$$
$$AB = 10$$

Since AB is equal to 10, answer choice A is correct.

Here is another one for you to try:

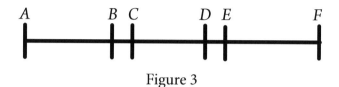

Figure 3

9. In Figure 3, $AC = 4\ cm$, $BE = 6\ cm$, and $DF = 4\ cm$. If BC and DE are both equal to 1 cm, then what is the total length, in cm, of segment AF?
    (A) 10
    (B) 11
    (C) 12
    (D) 13
    (E) 14

Our first step is to set up equations that break apart the segments into pieces.

$$AC = AB + BC = 4$$
$$BE = BC + CD + DE = 6$$
$$DF = DE + EF = 4$$

Now we can use the fact that BC and DE are both equal to 1 to solve for the other segments.

$$AC = AB + BC = AB + 1 = 4, \text{therefore } AB = 3$$
$$BE = BC + CD + DE = 1 + CD + 1 = 6, \text{therefore } CD = 4$$
$$DF = DE + EF = 1 + EF = 4, \text{therefore } EF = 3$$

Now let's look at the whole segment AF. We can rewrite it as a sum of its parts:

$$AF = AB + BC + CD + DE + EF$$

Now let's plug in what we know:

$$AF = AB + BC + CD + DE + EF = 3 + 1 + 4 + 1 + 3 = 12$$

Answer choice C is correct.

Creating and using inequalities

Sometimes you will see a word problem that uses the language "greater than" or "less than". These words let you know that you need to set up an inequality using the < or > sign.

- If you see "greater than" or "less than", use < or > sign

Once you set up an inequality, you can solve using the same rules that you use for solving for equations.

Here is an example of a problem that asks you to set up an inequality and then solve:

10. If $B + 7$ is greater than 10, then which of the following could NOT be B?
   (A) 2
   (B) 3 ½
   (C) 4
   (D) 5
   (E) 5 ½

If we set up the inequality, it would look like this:

$$B + 7 > 10$$

If we subtract 7 from both sides in order to get B by itself, we wind up with:

$$B > 3$$

Since B must be greater than 3, choice A could NOT work, so it is the correct answer.

Here is one for you to try:

11. If four times a number is greater than 12, then all of the following could be the number EXCEPT
   (A) 0
   (B) 3 ½
   (C) 4
   (D) 5 ½
   (E) 6

Let's start by setting up an inequality, using N to represent our number:

$4 \times N > 12$

Now we divide both sides by 4 in order to get N by itself. That leaves us with:

$N > 3$

Since the number has to be greater than 3, answer choice A could NOT be the number, so that is the correct answer.

Sometimes you will have to set up an inequality and then manipulate that inequality.

Let's look at this example:

12. If $Q + 3$ is less than 5, then $3 \times Q$ MUST be less than
   (A) 2
   (B) 3
   (C) 4
   (D) 5
   (E) 6

First, let's set up our inequality and solve:

$Q + 3 < 5$
$Q < 2$

Now we have to multiply both sides by 3 since we want to know what $3 \times Q$ is less than.

$3 \times Q < 3 \times 2$
$3 \times Q < 6$

Answer choice E is correct.

Here is one for you to try:

13. If $3 \times T$ is greater than 15, then $6 + T$ MUST be greater than
    (A) 9
    (B) 10
    (C) 11
    (D) 11 ½
    (E) 12

Let's set up our inequality and solve for the variable:

$3 \times T > 15$
$T > 5$

Now we have to find what $6 + T$ is greater than, so we add 6 to both sides. This gives us:

$T + 6 > 5 + 6$
$T + 6 > 11$

This tells us that $T + 6$ must be greater than 11, so answer choice C is correct.

Finally, let's look at a doozy of a question (if you are in fifth or sixth grade and can't even figure out what the question is asking, remember that percentile is what matters and percentile scores only compare you to other students your age!):

14. If K is greater than one, then which of the following could be equal to $10 \times K$?
    I. $\frac{1}{3}$
    II. 3.5
    III. 12

    (A) I only
    (B) II only
    (C) III only
    (D) I and II only
    (E) II and III only

The trick to this problem is that when we divide the number in the answer choice by 10, the result has to be greater than one since K is greater than one. If we divide $\frac{1}{3}$ by 10, we get $\frac{1}{30}$, which is definitely not greater than one, so I is out. If we divide 3.5 by 10, we get 0.35, which is also less than one, so II is out. If we divide 12 by 10, we get 1.2, which is greater than 1. So only III works. Answer choice C is correct.

Now you know the basics for solving equations on the SSAT. Be sure to complete the solving equations practice set.

Solving Equations Practice Set

1. If $J + 7 = 7$, then $J =$
   (A) 0
   (B) 17
   (C) 1
   (D) 7
   (E) 14

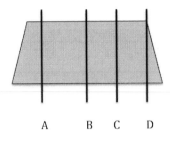

A   B   C   D

Figure 7

2. The shaded polygon in Figure 7 is divided by lines A, B, C, and D. The area of the shaded region between A and C is 40 and the area of the shaded region between B and D is 35. If the area between B and C is 15, what is the area of the shaded region between A and D?
   (A) 40
   (B) 45
   (C) 50
   (D) 55
   (E) 60

3. If R is less than 7, then $3R + 6$ could be
   (A) 26
   (B) 27
   (C) 28
   (D) 29
   (E) 30

4. If $P + 3$ is greater than 8, then $4 \times P$ MUST be greater than
   (A) 19
   (B) 20
   (C) 21
   (D) 25
   (E) 30

5. If $20 \times R = 20$, then $20 - R =$
    (A) 0
    (B) 1
    (C) 19
    (D) 20
    (E) 21

6. If $6 \times K + 5 = 10$, then $K =$
    (A) 0
    (B) $\frac{5}{6}$
    (C) $\frac{6}{5}$
    (D) $\frac{15}{6}$
    (E) 44

7. If $300 + b = 600$, then $600 + b =$
    (A) 0
    (B) 200
    (C) 300
    (D) 900
    (E) 1,200

8. Three short pipes are joined together to make one long pipe. Originally, each shorter piece of pipe was 10 feet long. When the pipes are joined together, however, the ends must overlap one another by one foot where they are connected. What is the length of the final, longer pipe?
    (A) 30 feet
    (B) 29 feet
    (C) 28 feet
    (D) 26 feet
    (E) 25 feet

9. If $10 \times L$ is less than one, then which of the following could be L?
    I. 3
    II. $1/2$
    III. 0

    (A) I only
    (B) I and II only
    (C) II and III only
    (D) III only
    (E) None of the above

10. If four times a number is greater than twelve, then all of the following could be the number EXCEPT
    (A) 5
    (B) 4 $1/2$
    (C) 4
    (D) 3 $1/2$
    (E) 3

Answers for Solving Equations Practice Set

1. A
2. E
3. A
4. B
5. C
6. B
7. D
8. C
9. D
10. E

Word Problems

The phrase "word problems" strikes fear into the heart of many students. On the SSAT, it doesn't have to!

Word problems on the SSAT tend to actually be very predictable. Identify the type of problem and you are halfway there.

The types of word problems that you are most likely to see on the SSAT are:

1. Word problems that require you to translate into equations and solve
2. Questions that ask you to form groups
3. Overlapping groups problems
4. Comparing individuals questions
5. Proportion (rate) problems

Some of these question types are really very easy, some of them are harder. As you work through these different problem types, think about how you can identify them on the actual test.

- Think about what makes each problem type unique

Word problems that require you to translate into equations and solve

The trick to this type of problem is not that the calculations are super hard, but rather that there are a lot of steps to follow. The key is to underline the information that you need to solve. For example, if a problem said "Jack's family had a garage with four vehicles in it." We don't need to know that it was a garage or that the garage belonged to Jack's family. We do need to know that there were four vehicles, so that is what we underline.

- Underline information needed to solve

If you get stuck, ask yourself if you have used all the numbers given. If not, then think about how you could use that information. The SSAT generally does not give you numbers in a problem that you do not need to use in order to solve. Also, if you can't figure out how to use information, start at the end of the problem and process the information as you move back to the beginning of the problem.

How to get unstuck:

- Use all numbers given in problem
- Start at the end of the question and work backwards

Here is what these questions look like on the SSAT:

1. Jane bought four packages of donut holes which each contained 15 donut holes. She ate two donut holes on the way to school. When she got to school, she gave three donut holes to each of her classmates. She had four donut holes left over. How many classmates does Jane have?
   (A) 15
   (B) 16
   (C) 18
   (D) 30
   (E) 45

To solve this problem, you first need to figure out how many donut holes she had to begin with. She had 4 packs of 15 each. The word "of" tells us to multiply, so we do 4×15, which gives us a total of 60 donut holes. She then ate 2 of them, so she had only 58 left. If you were to divide by 3 at this point, you wouldn't get an even number of students. So we have to go back and see what we missed. And we have to start at the end. If we look at the end of the problem, we can see that she had 4 donut holes left over. So she didn't divide 58 donut holes among her classmates, she divided 54 donut holes among her classmates. So we divide 54 by 3 and get that she had 18 classmates. Choice C is correct.

Here is one for you to try:

2. At the beginning of the year, Sam bought 3 boxes of pencils. Each of these boxes contained 18 pencils. He used 4 new pencils each week of school up until the holiday break. If he had ten pencils that had not been used when the holiday break began, then how many weeks were there between the start of school and the holiday break?
    (A) 10
    (B) 11
    (C) 12
    (D) 13
    (E) 14

To solve, let's first figure out how many pencils he started with. He had 3 boxes of 18, so we do 3×18 in order to get 54. Now we have to subtract off 10 since he had 10 pencils left at the end. That means that he used 44 new pencils. Since he used 4 pencils a week, we divide 44 by 4 and get that there must have been 11 weeks of school, so answer B is correct.

Another type of problem requires us to find a total and then divide.

Here is how it looks on the SSAT:

3. A certain restaurant charges $50 for a room rental and then $6 per attendee to host a party. If 10 guests come to a party and they share the cost equally, then how much should each person pay?
    (A) $6
    (B) $8
    (C) $10
    (D) $11
    (E) $20

Our first step is to figure out what the total cost of the party would be. It would cost $50 for the room rental but we also have to add the cost of the guests. Since there are 10 guests and each guest costs $6, then the total cost just for the guests would be $60. If we add in the room rental, the total cost would be $110. Since there are ten people sharing the cost equally, we divide $110 by 10 to get that each person would have to pay $11. Answer choice D is correct.

Here is another one for you to try:

4. To run in a race costs $16 for the first family member and $4 for each additional family member. If four family members all run in a race and split the cost equally, then how much would each person pay?
    (A) $16
    (B) $12
    (C) $10
    (D) $7
    (E) $4

If four family members ran, they would have to pay $16 for the first person and then a total of $12 for the next three people. This adds up to a total of $28. If we divide this equally among the four people, we get that each person would pay $7. Answer choice D is correct.

The next one is a little harder. Just remember to underline what is needed and to write down your work as you go. The more steps that a problem has, the more important it is to write down your work!

5. A baseball team plays 30 games in their season. So far, they have lost 12 games and won 5. How many of their remaining games must they win in order to win more than half their games this season?
    (A) 9
    (B) 10
    (C) 11
    (D) 13
    (E) 15

First of all, let's figure out how many games they have to win total. Since there are 30 games, they must win 15 of them in order to win half their games. However, the problem says that they want to win MORE than half their games. So they must win 16 games. They have already won 5, so they have to win 11 more in order to reach their goal. Answer choice C is correct.

Questions that ask you to form groups

Some questions will give you some rules about groups and then ask you about how many groups can be formed. Pay attention to the rules as well as whether they are asking for the number of groups possible, the least number of groups possible, or the greatest number of groups possible.

- Underline the rules for groups
- Circle it if they ask for the least number of groups or greatest number of groups

Here is how the questions could look on the test:

6. There are 15 people waiting in line at a restaurant. If there can be no more than 5 people at a table and no two tables can have the same number of people seated at them, what is the smallest number of tables needed to seat all 15 people?
   (A) 8
   (B) 10
   (C) 3
   (D) 2
   (E) 5

Let's start with plugging in answer choice D since it is the smallest. If we had two tables, one could have 5 people and one could have 4 people since no two tables can have the same number of people. This adds up to 9 people, so choice D does not work. Now let's try choice C since it is the next smallest answer choice. If we had 5 people at one table, 4 people at the next table, and 3 people at the last table, that would only add up to 12 people, which is not enough. Now we try choice E. The first table would have 5 people, the next table would have 4 people, the next table would have 3 people, the next table would have two people, and the last table would have 1 person. This adds up to 15, so choice E is correct.

Here is another one for you to try:

7. There are twenty students on a fieldtrip. They need to divide into groups. If each group must have at least 3 students but no more than six, what is the largest number of groups that the students can form?
   (A) 4
   (B) 3
   (C) 7
   (D) 6
   (E) 8

Since we are looking for the largest number, we want to make each group as small as possible. However, the problem tells us that we can't have less than three students in each group. Let's start with choice E since it is the largest. If we had 8 groups, then we wouldn't have enough students for each group to have at least 3 students (we would need 24 students to form 8 groups), so choice E is out. Now we try choice C and run into the same problem (we would need 21 students to form 7 groups). We don't have enough students so that each group would have atleast 3 people. If we try choice D, we would have enough students for each group to have at least 3 people, so choice D is correct.

Here is an even harder one. It is not tricky but there are a lot of steps.

8. At Sunrise Elementary there are four fifth-grade classes, each with 20 students in the class. The whole fifth grade is going on a fieldtrip and there are three buses. If every student must ride a bus and the number of students on any bus cannot outnumber the number of students on another bus by more than one, what is the greatest number of fifth grade students that can ride on any one bus?
   (A) 80
   (B) 60
   (C) 27
   (D) 26
   (E) 20

Our first step is to figure out how many fifth-grade students there are. If we do 4×20, then we get that there are a total of 80 students. Now we have to divide the number of students by the number of buses. If we do $80 \div 3$, we get that there are 26.6666 students per bus. But we can't have a partial person! This means that one bus would have 26 students and the other two buses would each have 27 students since there was a remainder of 2. The question asks what is the greatest number of students on any one bus, so choice C is correct.

Overlapping groups problems

There are two types of these questions:

1. Questions that give us two groups that overlap and ask by how much they overlap
2. Questions that give us two groups and one group fits inside the other group

The first type of question tells us how many people belong to two different groups and then tell us how many total people there are. If we add the two groups together, it is greater than the total number of people, so there must be some overlap in the two groups.

To solve these problems:

- Add the two groups together.
- From this number subtract the total number of people.
- This gives us the correct answer choice, or how many people belong to both groups.

Here is how the question can look on the SSAT:

9. In an elementary school, 400 students own a bike and 350 students own a scooter. If a total of 700 students own either a bike or a scooter or both, how many students must own both a bike and a scooter?
    (A) 0
    (B) 50
    (C) 75
    (D) 100
    (E) 300

To solve this problem, first we add the two groups together. That gives us 750 students. However, there are only 700 students who own either a bike or a scooter. If we subtract 700 from 750, we get that 50 students must own both a bike and a scooter, so answer choice B is correct.

Here is another one for you to try:

10. In a recent poll, 500 people were found to have either a brother or a sister or both. If 300 of these people had a brother and 350 of these people had a sister, then how many people have both a brother and a sister?
    (A) 50
    (B) 100
    (C) 150
    (D) 200
    (E) 300

If we add 300 and 350, we get 650. We then subtract 500 from this number and get 150. This means that 150 people must have both a brother and a sister, so choice C is correct.

The second type of overlapping groups questions gives us two groups and one group fits entirely inside of the other group. We have to use the difference between the two groups to see how many people are in that in between group.

Here is an example:

11. In a certain class, 14 students travel at least 2 miles to get to school. In the same class, 5 students travel more than 5 miles to get to school. How many students in this class travel at least 2 miles but less than 5 miles to get to school?
    (A) 19
    (B) 14
    (C) 12
    (D) 9
    (E) 7

Since 14 students travel at least 2 miles, this group would include students that travel more than 5 miles. To find out how many students travel more than 2 miles but less than 5 miles, we subtract the "more than five miles" group from the "at least 2 miles" group. This gives us 14 − 5 = 9, so answer choice D is correct.

Here is another one to try:

12. In a class of 21 students, all of the students missed at least one question on a test. If 16 students missed three or more questions, how many students missed one or two questions?
    (A) 5
    (B) 6
    (C) 9
    (D) 16
    (E) 21

The whole group is 21 students, and this includes the group that missed three or more questions. To find just the group that missed one or two questions, we have to subtract off the students who missed three or more. This gives us 21 − 16 = 5, so answer choice A is correct.

Comparing individuals questions

Comparing individual questions give you a bunch of comparisons and you have to sort out an order for the whole group. For example, they might tell you who is taller than whom, or who is older than whom, and so on. The trick to these is simply to draw out the orders given.

- Make a simple drawing for comparison

Here is an example:

13. In a bicycle race, George finished 3 meters behind Carl. Sarah finished ahead of George but behind Hal. Lori finished 5 meters ahead of George. Who came in LAST?
(A) Sarah
(B) George
(C) Carl
(D) Lori
(E) Cannot be determined

The trick to this question is to draw it out:

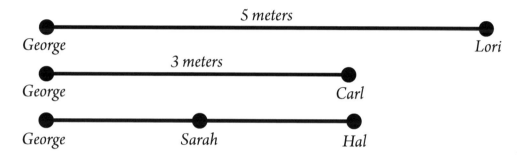

From this we can see that George always comes in last. We can't tell who came in first, or the order of the other bikers, but George always finishes last, so choice B is correct.

Here is another question to try:

14. Chuck is older than Lance but younger than Milo. Taylor is older than both Chuck and Lance. Who is the THIRD oldest?
(A) Chuck
(B) Lance
(C) Milo
(D) Taylor
(E) Cannot be determined

Let's go ahead and draw it out:

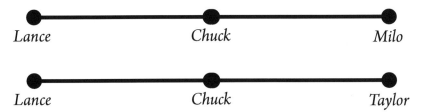

From this drawing, we can see that both Milo and Taylor are older than Chuck. We can't tell who is oldest, but the question does not ask for that. We can tell that Chuck is the third oldest, however, so choice A is correct.

Proportion Questions (Rate)

These questions often use the word "rate". They can also use the words "per" or "for each".

- Look out for the words "rate", "per", and "for each"

Essentially, what these questions are asking you to do is set up equivalent fractions, or proportions.

Here is an example:

15. When a school goes on a fieldtrip, they need 2 chaperones for each group of 15 students. If there are a total of 105 students going on a fieldtrip, then how many chaperones do they need?
    (A) 7
    (B) 9
    (C) 14
    (D) 15
    (E) 30

In order to solve this problem, we set up equivalent fractions:

$$\frac{2 \text{ chaperones}}{15 \text{ students}} = \frac{x \text{ chaperones}}{105 \text{ students}}$$

Now we have to solve for x. To get from 15 to 105, we have to multiply by 7. Since we multiplied the denominator by 7, we also have to multiply the numerator by 7. This gives us $2 \times 7 = 14$, so answer choice C is correct.

Here is another one to try. It is a little trickier, but just remember to keep in mind what they are asking for.

16. Suzy works at a museum where she is supposed to give out 3 brochures for every 10 people who come through the door. She started the day with 200 brochures. If 150 people came through the door that day, how many brochures should she have had remaining when the museum closed?
(A) 30
(B) 45
(C) 150
(D) 155
(E) 200

First we need to figure out how many brochures she should have handed out. We can use equivalent fractions to do that:

$$\frac{3 \ brochures}{10 \ visitors} = \frac{x \ brochures}{150 \ visitors}$$

We had to multiply the denominator by 15 to get from 10 to 150. This means that we have to multiply the numerator by 15 as well. That tells us that 45 brochures were given out. We aren't done yet, though, since we need to know how many brochures were remaining. We need to do $200 - 45 = 155$, to get that there were 155 brochures left over so answer choice D is correct.

Some rate question require you to convert between minutes and hours. Just remember to do the conversion!

$1 \ hour = 60 \ minutes$

Here is one for you to try:

17. Jim runs four laps every six minutes. At this rate, how many laps does Jim run in one hour?
    (A) 10
    (B) 24
    (C) 40
    (D) 54
    (E) 60

To solve this problem, set up equivalent fractions:

$$\frac{4\ laps}{6\ minutes} = \frac{x\ laps}{1\ hour}$$

The problem here is that we are using minutes and trying to get to hours. Let's convert that one hour into 60 minutes:

$$\frac{4\ laps}{6\ minutes} = \frac{x\ laps}{60\ minutes}$$

To get from 6 to 60, we multiply by 10. So we must also multiply the numerator by 10. That gives us $4 \times 10 = 40$ laps, so answer choice C is correct.

Here is another problem that requires us to convert between minutes and hours:

18. Bill took a 6-mile bike ride. He rode the first mile in 4 minutes. If he continued to ride at the same rate, what fractional part of an hour did it take for him to ride the entire six miles?
    (A) ⅙
    (B) ⅕
    (C) ⅖
    (D) ½
    (E) ¾

First we have to figure out how many minutes his ride took using equivalent fractions:

$$\frac{1\ mile}{4\ minutes} = \frac{6\ miles}{x\ minutes}$$

We had to multiply the numerator by 6 to get to 6 miles, so we must also multiply the bottom by 6. This gives us that the whole ride took 24 minutes. Now we have to figure out what part of an hour is 24 minutes. We can set up a fraction and then reduce:

$$\frac{24\ minutes}{60\ minutes} = \frac{24 \div 12}{60 \div 12} = \frac{2}{5}$$

Answer choice C is correct.

Now you know what you need to answer word problems on the SSAT. Be sure to complete the word problems practice set!

Word Problems Practice Set

1. At the batting cage, 18 buckets had more than 14 balls in each bucket. If 10 of those buckets had at least 16 balls in each bucket, then how many buckets had exactly 15 balls in them?
    (A) 4
    (B) 6
    (C) 8
    (D) 9
    (E) 11

2. Carol is shorter than Jim but taller than Mallory. If Harold is taller than both Carol and Mallory, who is the tallest?
    (A) Carol
    (B) Jim
    (C) Mallory
    (D) Harold
    (E) Cannot be determined

3. Sharon took a 4-mile jog. If she jogged the first mile in 9 minutes, then if she continued at the same rate, what fraction of an hour did her jog take?
    (A) ⅓
    (B) ⅖
    (C) ⁷⁄₁₂
    (D) ⅗
    (E) ⅘

4. A golfer is playing 18 holes. She has won 7 holes and lost 3 holes. What is the greatest number of holes that she can lose on the rest of the course and still beat her opponent?
    (A) 4
    (B) 5
    (C) 7
    (D) 8
    (E) 9

5. Lisa bought three packs of gum that each contained 15 sticks of gum. She chewed one piece of gum and then gave each of her friends 3 pieces each. She had two pieces of gum left at after this. How many friends did Lisa give three pieces of gum to?
   (A) 14
   (B) 15
   (C) 17
   (D) 20
   (E) 32

6. A carriage ride costs $12 for the first two people and $4 more for each additional person. If four people go on a carriage ride together and split the cost equally, how much would each person pay?
   (A) $4
   (B) $5
   (C) $6
   (D) $12
   (E) $20

7. At a high school, there are 3 homeroom classes, each with 15 students in them. These classes need to divide themselves among 4 lunch tables. If the number of students sitting at any lunch table cannot outnumber the number of students sitting at another lunch table by more than one, what is the least number of students that could be sitting at any one table?
   (A) 1
   (B) 2
   (C) 9
   (D) 11
   (E) 12

8. Josh planted 600 trees on five acres. He was only supposed to plant 15 trees per acre, however. How many trees should he remove?
   (A) 525
   (B) 500
   (C) 300
   (D) 150
   (E) 75

9. A carwash can wash 3 cars every ten minutes. At this rate, how many cars can the carwash clean in one hour?
   (A) 3
   (B) 10
   (C) 18
   (D) 30
   (E) 60

10. In a long jump competition, George jumped 2 meters further than Frances. Corrie jumped further than George, but not as far as Megan. If Kim jumped 3 meters further than Frances, but not as far as Corrie, who jumped the THIRD farthest?
    (A) George
    (B) Corrie
    (C) Megan
    (D) Kim
    (E) Cannot be determined

11. A machine stamps 300 notebook covers every 12 minutes. At that rate, how long will it take the machine to stamp 1,050 notebooks?
    (A) 36 minutes
    (B) 42 minutes
    (C) 60 minutes
    (D) 1 hour 6 minutes
    (E) 1 hour 10 minutes

Answers to Word Problems Practice Set

1. C
2. E
3. D
4. B
5. A
6. B
7. D
8. A
9. C
10. D
11. B

Geometry

On the SSAT, the geometry section deals mostly with angles and shapes and their measurements.

In this section, we will cover:

- Definition of a polygon and how to find its perimeter
- Area of rectangular shapes
- Cube or prism questions
- Angles
- Triangles and their properties
- Circles

Polygons

The root "poly" means many, so a polygon is a many-sided shape. Remember that a circle is not considered a polygon.

- Triangles, rectangles, pentagons and hexagons are examples of polygons

You won't need to define a polygon on the test, but you will need to be able to recognize one.

Perimeter

The perimeter of a polygon is the measurement of the outside of a polygon. You find the perimeter of a polygon by adding up the lengths of all the sides.

- The formula for the perimeter is $P = s + s + s + s$ depending on how many sides the polygon has.

For example, if the lengths of the sides of a rectangle are 4, 6, 4, and 6, the perimeter is $P = 4 + 6 + 4 + 6 = 20$.

- If you are given just the length and the width of a rectangle, multiply each by 2 and then add those numbers together to find the perimeter

On the test you may be given all the measurements needed to calculate the perimeter. However, the test writers might also give you the perimeter and ask you to calculate side lengths.

Here is an example of how these concepts may be tested:

1. If the perimeter of a square is 4 cm, then what is the length of each side?
   (A) 4 cm
   (B) 3 cm
   (C) 2 cm
   (D) 1 cm
   (E) ½ cm

We know that a square has four sides that are all the same length. This means that we can divide 4 cm by 4 sides and we get that each side is 1 cm long. Answer choice D is correct.

Here is another problem for you to try:

2. If the perimeter of a triangle whose sides are all the same length is 2 cm, then what is the length of each side?
   (A) 3 cm
   (B) 2 cm
   (C) ⅔ cm
   (D) ½ cm
   (E) ⅓ cm

This problem is a little trickier because the length of each of the sides is not a whole number. There are three equal sides, so we have to divide 2 cm into three equal pieces. We get ⅔ cm for each side. Answer choice C is correct.

Sometimes the test writers may give you a figure where not all of the side lengths are given and then ask you to find the perimeter. In this case, you first have to find missing side lengths.

- If the test gives you a figure with side lengths and asks for the perimeter, first check to make sure that you have all the side lengths and solve for any side lengths that you do not have

Here is what these perimeter problems look like on the SSAT:

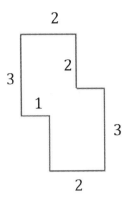

3. All angles in the figure above are right angles. What is the perimeter of the figure?
   (A) 11
   (B) 12
   (C) 13
   (D) 14
   (E) 16

The trick to this problem is that not all the sides are given. To find the perimeter of the figure, we first have to figure out some of the side lengths. From the bottom vertical pieces, we can add the segment lengths to figure out that the width of the figure would be 3 (1 + 2 = 3). That means that the unlabeled segment on the right has to be 1. From the right side of the figure, we can add the segment lengths to figure out that the height of the figure is 5 (3 + 2 = 5), so we can see that the unlabeled segment on the left must be 2. Now we just add all of our segment lengths together to get 16, or choice E.

Here is an example of a problem that asks you to use the idea of perimeter- even though the word "perimeter" does not even show up in the question:

4. Kyle is winding a piece of string around pegs on a pegboard, as shown below. Kyle starts at *A* and winds the string in a clockwise direction (as shown). If the string is 87 cm long, then the string will run out just after passing which peg?
   (A) A
   (B) B
   (C) C
   (D) D
   (E) E

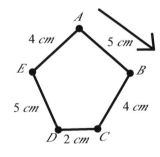

To solve this problem, we first have to figure out what the perimeter of the figure is. If we add the sides together, we get 4 + 5 + 4 + 2 + 5 = 20 cm. Since the string is 87 cm long, we know that it must go around the board more than once. If it goes around once, then 20 cm has been used up, if it goes around twice, then 40 cm has been used. From this we can see that one more time would give us 60 cm and then another full rotation would get us to 80 cm. This tells us that the string passed point A at 80 cm and there are now 7 cm left. This 7 cm would allow Kyle to pass point B, but does not provide enough string to get to point C. Therefore, the string will run out just after passing peg B and answer choice B is correct.

Area of rectangular shapes

The area of a rectangle is the amount of space taken up by the inside of the shape.

- The formula for the area of a rectangle is $A = l \times w$, where l is the length and w is the width.

If you have a rectangle that is 4 inches by 6 inches, we can calculate the area to be $A = 4 \times 6 = 24$ inches.

Remember that a square is a special rectangle.

- The formula for the area of a square is $A = s \times s = s^2$, where s is the length of one side.

Area problems tend to show up at the end of the math section. Remember that most students do not get these last questions correct and that the score that matters is your percentile, which only compares you to other students your age. So do your best on these problems, but don't sweat it too much if they seem over your head! Particularly if you are in 5th or 6th grade.

Here is an example of how these concepts may be tested:

5. In figure 2, MNOP is a square MQRP is a rectangle. If the length of PR is 10 and the length of NQ is 3, then what is the area of square MNOP?
    (A) 7
    (B) 10
    (C) 28
    (D) 49
    (E) 100

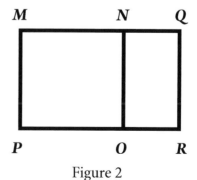

Figure 2

The first step for this problem is to figure out what the length is of one side of the square. We know that the length of PR must be the same as the length of MQ. This means that the length of MQ must be 10. We also know that the length of NQ is 3. If we subtract the length of NQ from the length of MQ, we get that the length of MN must be 7. Since the area of the square is equal to the side of a length squared (or multiplied by itself), we know that the area of square MNOP must be 49, or answer choice D.

Here is another example of an area problem on the SSAT:

6. The large square in Figure 3 has four smaller squares within it. The area of each smaller square is 5. What is the area of the shaded region?

(A) 5
(B) 7 ½
(C) 10
(D) 12 ½
(E) 15

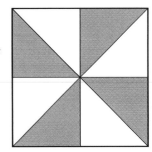

Figure 3

Each of the shaded triangles takes up half of a small square. We know that the area of each small square is 5, so the area of each triangle must be 2 ½. There are four of the shaded triangles, so we multiply 4 times 2 ½, which gives us 10. Answer choice C is correct.

Cubes and prisms

There are not a lot of prism and cube problems on the Middle Level SSAT, but you may see some. Think of a rectangular prism as being the shape of your standard cardboard box. A cube is a rectangular prism whose sides are all the same length and width (think of dice).

You don't need to know a lot of complicated formulas for volume on the SSAT. You may need to know the volume of a cube, however.

The volume of a cube is always calculated as $V = s^3$ where s is the length of one of the sides.

A classic problem involves fitting small cubes into a larger cube.

Here is an example:

7. The small cube below is 1 inch on all sides. How many cubes of this size would be required to fill a larger cube that is 2 inches on all sides?

   (A) 2
   (B) 4
   (C) 8
   (D) 16
   (E) 32

Technique 1: Think of the cube having to be doubled in all 3 dimensions. It must be twice as wide, twice as long, and twice as high. Therefore, the 2-inch cube will be 8 times as big, and thus would need 8 smaller cubes. Answer choice C is correct.

Technique 2: Another way to think of the problem is to compare the volumes of the two cubes. The volume of the small cube is $1 \times 1 \times 1 = 1$ in^3. The volume of the 2-inch cube is $2 \times 2 \times 2 = 8$ in^3. The larger cube has 8 times the volume of the smaller cube. Again, answer choice C is correct.

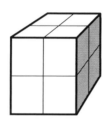

Use whichever technique feels easier for you to use.

Some problems require you to visualize how 3-D objects can fit together.

Here is another example of a problem that requires you to fit smaller cubes with a larger prism.

8. Figure 4 below shows a block that is made up of smaller cubes. How may cubes were needed to make this block?
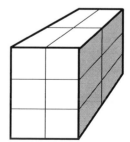
   (A) 6
   (B) 8
   (C) 10
   (D) 12
   (E) 14

For this question, we have to be able to picture the blocks that we can not see. We can count that the front layer has six blocks in it. We can then see that there are two of these layers going back. This means that we can do $6 \times 2 = 12$ to get the total number of blocks. Answer choice D is correct.

Here is an example of a problem that you need to be able to see things in 3-D in order to solve:

9. In Figure 5, a rectangular wooden block is shown with dimensions. If Ally cut the block into two rectangular blocks of exactly the same size and shape, which of the following could be the dimensions of each of the smaller wooden blocks, given in centimeters?

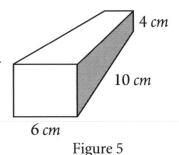

Figure 5

   (A) $6 \times 10 \times 2$
   (B) $6 \times 5 \times 2$
   (C) $3 \times 5 \times 2$
   (D) $3 \times 5 \times 4$
   (E) $3 \times 10 \times 2$

The key to solving this problem is being able to visualize the different ways that the block could be cut. The most obvious way to cut the block would be the slice it right down the middle on the 10 cm side. This would give us two blocks, each with the dimensions of $6 \times 5 \times 4$. The problem is that this is not an answer choice. So we have to think of how else the block could be cut. To get an answer choice, we actually have to picture slicing the block sideways, or cutting the 4 cm side in half. This gives us two blocks with dimensions $6 \times 10 \times 2$, so answer choice A is correct.

Angles

An angle is where 2 lines or line segments meet.

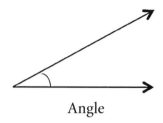

Angle

Here are some important facts about angles:

- A right angle has 90°
- A straight angle has 180°
- Opposite angles are equal

A right angle looks like this:

We designate a right angle like this:

The little box is the symbol to tell you that the angle measure is 90°, which is a right angle.

A straight angle is just a straight line. So why does it have an angle measure of 180°?? Well, here is the straight line: _____

Now, put a line down the middle: _____

Now you see that it is made up of 2 right angles, each measuring 90°, so the total is 180°. Remember, a straight angle has 180°.

Here is an example of how this could be tested on the SSAT:

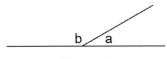

Figure 6

10. In the figure above, angle a measures 50°. What is the measure of angle b?
    (A) 40°
    (B) 50°
    (C) 100°
    (D) 130°
    (E) Cannot be determined

A straight line has 180°, so $(a + b) = 180$

If we plug in what is given and solve, we get:

$(50 + b) = 180$
$b = 130°$

Answer choice D is correct.

Now let's look at opposite angles:

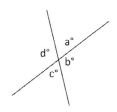

Angles a and c are equal to each other. Angles b and d are also equal to one another.

Here is how this concept could be tested on the SSAT:

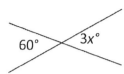

Figure not drawn to scale

11. In the figure above, what is the value of *x*?
   (A) 15
   (B) 20
   (C) 50
   (D) 60
   (E) 180

We know that opposite angles are equal, so we know that *3x=60*. If we solve for *x*, we get that it is equal to 20, or answer choice B.

Triangles

There are several types of triangles:

- An equilateral triangle has all 3 sides equal, and all 3 angles are the same.
- An isosceles triangle has 2 equal sides and the angles opposite those sides are equal.
- A right triangle has one 90° angle, which is called a right angle. The sum of the other 2 angles is 90°.

Another important fact about triangles is this:

- The sum of the 3 angles in any triangle is always 180°.

Here is how these concepts could be tested on the SSAT:

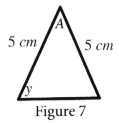

Figure 7

12. In the triangle in Figure 7, the measure of angle A is 80 degrees. What is the angle measure of y in degrees?
    (A) 40
    (B) 45
    (C) 50
    (D) 80
    (E) It cannot be determined from the information given.

We can identify this triangle as an isosceles triangle because we are given two sides of the same length. The angles opposite these sides are equal. Since we know that the sum of the angles in a triangle equal 180 degrees, we can determine the value of y, eliminating answer choice E. The sum of the two unknown angles is $180° - 80° = 100°$. Divide this by 2 and $\frac{100°}{2} = 50°$. The correct answer is choice C.

Here is another one for you to try:

13. In figure 8 below, what is the value of *w*?
    (A) 15°
    (B) 30°
    (C) 45°
    (D) 90°
    (E) Cannot be determined

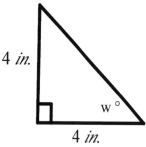

4 *in.*

w °

4 *in.*

Figure 8

To answer this question, you first need to recognize that we are dealing with an isosceles right triangle. Any time we see a triangle with two sides that are the same length, it almost always means that we will need to use the fact that this makes the triangle isosceles. If a triangle is isosceles, this means that the two angles opposite the congruent sides will also be congruent. We know that the angles in a triangle add up to 180° and since one of the angles is 90°, then the remaining two angles must add up to 90°. Since these two angles are also equal to one another, we simply divide 90° by 2 and get that each angle is 45°. Answer choice C is correct.

Area of a triangle

The area of a triangle is the space inside a triangle. The formula is $A = \frac{1}{2}bh$. In a right triangle, like the one below, this formula is easy to use.

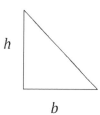

h

b

When the triangle is not a right triangle, you have to draw in the height as shown in the triangles below.

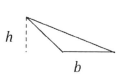

h

b

h

b

The same formula is used here, although you may need to determine the height from other information given about the triangle.

- The formula for area of a triangle is $A = \frac{1}{2}bh$.

Here is an example of how these concepts may be tested:

14. What is the area of the shaded region if *ABCD* is a square?

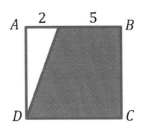

    (A) 7

    (B) 14

    (C) 42

    (D) 49

    (E) It cannot be determined from the information given.

Although all the dimensions of the shaded region are not given, we can use the information about the square and the triangle to solve this problem, so choice (E) can be eliminated. First, find the area of the square. The length of AB is *2+5=7*. The area of a square is $A=s^2$, so the area of square *ABCD* is $A=s^2=7^2=49$. Since the area we are looking for is smaller than this, we can eliminate choice D. Next, calculate the area of the triangle. Side *AD=AB*, so the area of the triangle is $A=\frac{1}{2}bh=\frac{1}{2}(2)(7)=7$. Eliminate answer choice (A). Now, subtract the area of the triangle from the area of the square to find the area of the shaded region, *A=49–7=42*. The correct answer is choice (C).

Circles

On the Middle Level SSAT, you basically need to be able to use the concepts of radius and diameter. The radius is the distance from the center to the edge of the circle. The diameter is the distance straight across the circle, going through the center. The diameter is twice the radius.

- Radius= distance from center of circle to any point on circle
- Diameter=distance straight across a circle, through the center
- Diameter= 2 × radius

Here is an example of a question that tests these concepts:

15. Figure 9 shows a circle with a radius of 5. Which of the following could NOT be the length of a line segment that lies completely within the circle?

    (A) 11

    (B) 10

    (C) 8

    (D) 5

    (E) 4

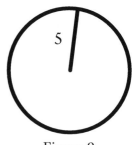

Figure 9

The longest line segment that will fit completely inside a circle is the diameter. In this circle, the diameter is 10. That means that any line segment that is longer than 10 would not fit entirely within the circle. Answer choice A is correct.

Here is another example of a question that tests the concept of diameter:

16. Fifteen baseballs are packed in a box as shown in Figure 10. Every ball touches another ball or the side of the box in four spots. The diameter of each baseball is 3 inches. Which of the following is possible for the length and width of the box?
    (A) $3\ in \times 5\ in$
    (B) $6\ in \times 10\ in$
    (C) $6\ in \times 12\ in$
    (D) $9\ in \times 12\ in$
    (E) $9\ in \times 15\ in$

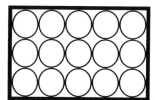

Figure 10

The diameter of each ball is 3 inches. Since there are 5 balls across, we know that one side of the box must be at least 15 inches. There are 3 balls going up and down, so we know that the other side of the box needs to be at least 9 inches. Answer choice E is correct.

Now you know what you need in order to crush the geometry questions on the SSAT! Be sure to complete the geometry practice set that follows.

Geometry Practice Set

1. In Figure 1 above, what is the value of x?
   (A) 8
   (B) 15
   (C) 20
   (D) 30
   (E) 60

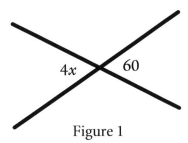

Figure 1

2. The cube in Figure 2 is 2 inches on all sides. How many cubes of this size would be required to fit into a larger cube that is 4 inches on all sides?
   (A) 8
   (B) 16
   (C) 32
   (D) 64
   (E) 128

Figure 2

3. In the triangle to the side, what is the value of x?
   (A) 4
   (B) 6
   (C) 8
   (D) 10
   (E) Cannot be determined

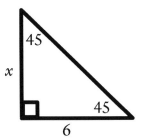

4. What is the area of the quadrilateral ABCD in Figure 3?
   (A) 11
   (B) 12
   (C) 15
   (D) 27
   (E) Cannot be determined

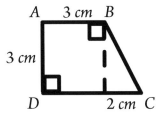

Figure 3

5. If the perimeter of a square is 5 inches, what is the length of each side?
   (A) $\frac{1}{5}$ inch
   (B) $\frac{1}{2}$ inch
   (C) 1 inch
   (D) $1\frac{1}{4}$ inches
   (E) $1\frac{1}{2}$ inches

6. Lance is winding a strong around the pegboard in Figure 4. He starts at P and winds the string in the counter clockwise direction (as shown). If the string is 60 cm long, Lance will run out of string directly after passing which peg?

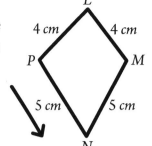

Figure 4

(A) L
(B) M
(C) N
(D) P
(E) Cannot be determined

7. The square in Figure 5 has 4 smaller squares within it, as shown. If the area of each of the smaller squares is 5, then what is the area of the shaded region?

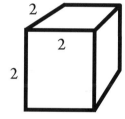

Figure 5

(A) 4
(B) 5
(C) 7.5
(D) 10
(E) 12.5

8. The wooden block in Figure 6 is to be cut into 8 equally sized cubes. What will be the dimensions of each of these cubes?

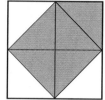

Figure 6

(A) $8 \times 8 \times 8$
(B) $2 \times 2 \times 2$
(C) $2 \times 2 \times 1$
(D) $2 \times 1 \times 1$
(E) $1 \times 1 \times 1$

Answers to Geometry Practice Set

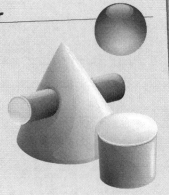

1. B
2. A
3. B
4. B
5. D
6. C
7. E
8. E

Visualization Problems

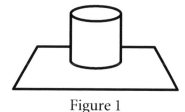

On the SSAT, you may have to visualize what COULD be.

There are few different problem types that require you to do this. In this section we will cover:

- Converting 3-D drawings to 2-D
- Questions that require you to think of possibilities
- Looking for patterns

Sometimes you have to see beyond what is on the paper, and you have to think and visualize, and sometimes use your pencil, in order to get the problem right.

The key to these problems is to NOT just jump on the first answer that looks right! These problems stretch your thinking and often the quick answer that you jump on is not the right one.

For these problems, you ALWAYS will look at all 5 answer choices before you answer the question

Converting 3-D drawing to 2-D

One type of problem that you should be familiar with is the 3-D (3 dimensional) to 2-D (2 dimensional) type. You are given a 3-D object and you have to decide what a part of it looks like in 2-D.

Here is an example of what this type of problem looks like:

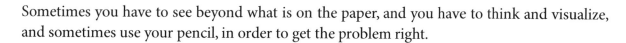

Figure 1

1. A cylindrical container of oatmeal with a flat bottom rests on a piece of paper, as shown in Figure 1 (on the previous page). Which of the following best represents the set of points where the container touches the paper?

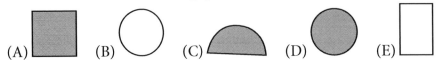

(A) (B) (C) (D) (E)

Think about the bottom of a flat cylindrical container such as an oatmeal box or a container of salt. Imagine setting it on a piece of paper. First, you know that where it touches the paper it will be a circle. This eliminates choices A and E. You can eliminate choice C because it is only half a circle. So now look at B and D. Answer B might be your first quick choice, and it is wrong! The bottom of the container is perfectly flat, so it touches the paper at the circle, PLUS all the points inside the circle, too. Therefore, the correct answer is D.

Here is another one for you to try:

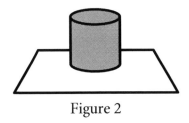

Figure 2

2. A cylindrical plastic cup is placed upside down on a piece of paper so that only its rim touches the paper, as shown in Figure 2. Which of the following shows all the points at which the cup touches the piece of paper?

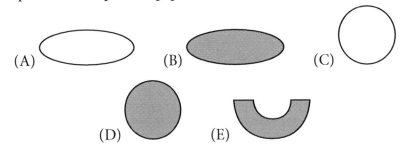

(A) (B) (C) (D) (E)

To solve this problem, we have to think about what a cup would look like in two dimensions. In Figure 2, it looks like the rim would be an oval, but that is only because it is a 3-D drawing showing depth. In two dimensions, the rim of the cup would actually be a circle, so we know it has to be choice C or D. Now, we have to make sure that we use all the information given in the problem. The problem tells us that only the rim of the cup touches the piece of paper so choice C is correct.

Questions that require you to think of possibilities

The next type of problem deals with visualizing limits and considering ALL of the possibilities of what can happen. Sometimes it is a word problem and sometimes it is a picture problem. The rules for this type of problem are:

1. Use your pencil AND your brain! Draw the problem out.
2. Read every word of the problem. There are hints about how to answer it.
3. Consider EVERY answer choice and think, before you mark your answer.

Let's try an example:

3. A cow is tied to a fencepost in the middle of a 60-foot fence. The rope is 20 feet long. What are the size and shape of his grazing area?

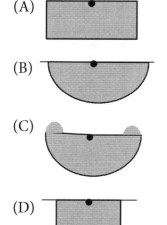

Get your pencil out for this one! Draw the post and the fence, and then draw the rope.

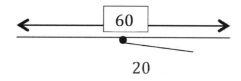

Now, act like a hungry cow. You are at the end of the rope. If you keep the rope tight, the pattern will be circular, so choices A and D are eliminated. Notice that the rope is shorter than the length of half the fence, so the cow can't get around the fence to graze on the other side, so choice C is out. This leaves choices B and E. If you quickly chose choice B, then you made the fatal decision for this type of problem! Notice that choice B allows the cow to eat almost to the very end of the 60-foot fence, whereas choice E restricts her from being too close to the end of the fence. The rope is 20 feet long, so the cow can't get very close to the end of the fence and choice E is correct.

Here is another one for you to try:

4. If points A and B were connected in the following figures, in which answer choice would a rectangle and a triangle be formed?

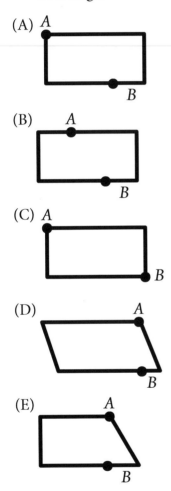

For this question, get out your pencil and connect A and B on each drawing. You also need to pay close attention to the question. The question tells us that we have to create a rectangle AND a triangle. The only answer choice that creates both a rectangle and a triangle when you connect A and B is choice D, so that is the correct answer choice.

Looking for patterns

The third type of problem that requires visualization involves patterns. A simple example is to see what happens if you turn a shape upside down. See what happens when you turn this triangle upside down:

That was easy. Now see what happens when you turn a shape upside down and then flip it sideways:

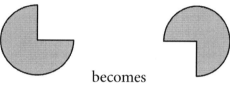

It's a little bit harder now!

The key to this type of problem is to do some self-talk. Ask yourself: "How does the first item become the second item, and what steps did they take to get there?" Then talk to yourself about it! For the pie shape above, there are TWO things that were done to it. First, they turned it upside down, so that the empty part was on the bottom right. Then they flipped it sideways, so then the empty part was flipped from the bottom right to the bottom left.

Here is an example of what a pattern question may look like on the SSSAT:

5.

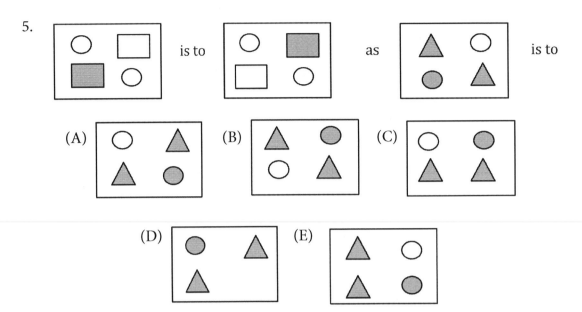

This problem checks to see that your brain can see the pattern when something is changed. In the pattern introduced in the question, the circles didn't change shape, position, or shading. The only thing that changed was that the shaded rectangles switched position. So do the same thing to the new figure. Keep the shaded triangles where they are, and then switch the 2 circles so that the shaded circle is now on the upper right. Answer choice B is the correct one.

Here is another one for you to try:

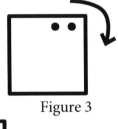

Figure 3

6. The square card in Figure 3 has had two holes punched in it, as shown. If the card is rotated in a clockwise direction, as shown, which of the following could NOT be what the card looks like?

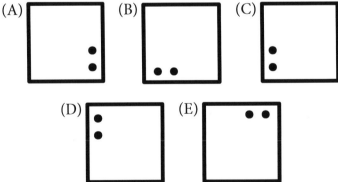

This question asks us to figure out what a figure would look like if we rotated it. The easiest thing to do is to pick up the paper and actually rotate it. What does the figure look like if you rotate the paper 90 degrees? What does it look like if you rotate it 180 degrees? If you do this, you can see that no matter who far you rotate the figure, you are not going to be able to get answer choice C. Since we are looking for the one that does NOT work, answer choice C is the correct answer.

Now you know the basics for visualizations problems. The best way to get good at these problems is just to practice them, so be sure to complete the visualization practice set.

Visualization Practice Set

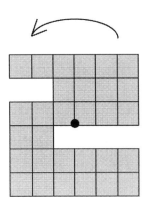

1. Given the figure above, if it rotates a quarter turn in the counterclockwise direction, which of the following would be the result?

(A)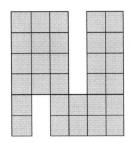

(B)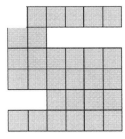

(C)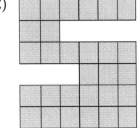

(D)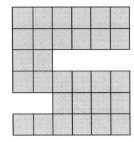

(E)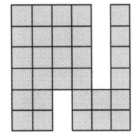

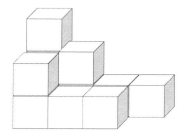

2. Given the figure above, how many small cubes were used to create this figure?
   (A) 7
   (B) 8
   (C) 9
   (D) 10
   (E) 11

3. Which of the following figures could be drawn without either lifting the pencil or retracing?

   (A)  (B) 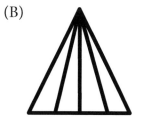 (C)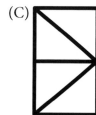

   (D) 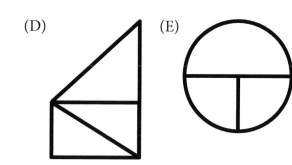 (E)

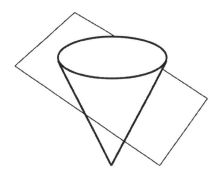

4. A plane slices through the cone-shaped object as shown above. What is the shape of the figure where the cone and the plane intersect?

(A) △   (B) ◯   (C) ⌣   (D) ⋁   (E) ⬭

Answers to Visualization Practice Set

1. A
2. E
3. D
4. E

Graphs

On the SSAT you will encounter several types of graphs that you will have to answer questions about. You may see a line graph, a bar graph, or a circle graph.

In this section we will cover:

1. Basic line graph and bar graph questions
2. More complex bar graphs
3. Circle graphs

The good news is that you will not have complicated math to do. The bad news is that you will have to read each question very carefully. That is the key to succeeding with these problems.

Common phrases and what they mean:

- "How many more…" means subtract
- "What percent of…" means find a percent
- "What is the difference…" means subtract
- "What fraction of…" means find a fraction
- "The greatest increase is…" means subtract
- "The combined total of…" means add

Basic line graph and bar graph questions

The trick to these question types is to read the question carefully. There are often two or three questions that go with the same graph, and they sometimes look a lot alike. The key is to look for the differences in the questions.

Here is an example of a line graph problem on the SSAT:

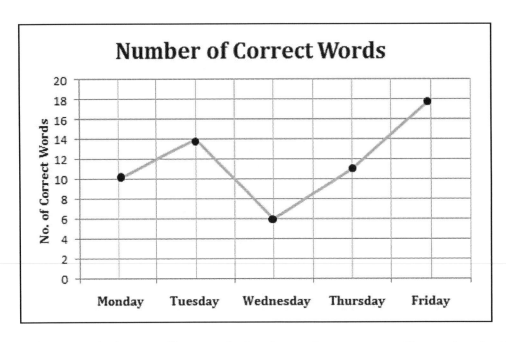

Elena is studying vocabulary wordlists. Each day she studies a new wordlist, and each night she takes a test to see how many words she has learned that day. Here are her results for last week.

1. During what 2-day period did the largest change in number of correct words occur?
   (A) Monday to Tuesday
   (B) Tuesday to Wednesday
   (C) Wednesday to Thursday
   (D) Thursday to Friday
   (E) None of these

Notice that the question is about change. It doesn't ask about improvement, so even a 'negative' answer will be possible. Let's look at each period:

Monday to Tuesday: 10 to 14, so the change is 4
Tuesday to Wednesday: 14 to 6, so the change is 8
Wednesday to Thursday: 6 to 11, so the change is 5
Thursday to Friday: 11 to 18, so the change is 7

The greatest change is from Tuesday to Wednesday so answer choice B is correct.

Here is another question that uses the same graph:

2. The number of words learned on Wednesday is how many times the number of words learned on Friday?
    (A) 18
    (B) 6
    (C) 3
    (D) ⅓
    (E) ⅙

The first thing that you need to note about this question is that it is asking for how many times and not how many more. This means that we are looking for what we need to multiply the words learned on Friday by in order to get the words learned on Wednesday. On Friday, Elena learned 18 words and on Wednesday she learned 6 words. In order to from 18 to 6, you have to multiply ⅛ by ⅓ to get to 6 so answer choice D is correct.

The next type of graph you will see is a bar chart, where the height of the bar shows how many times something happened or how many there are of some category.

Here is an example of a bar chart question:

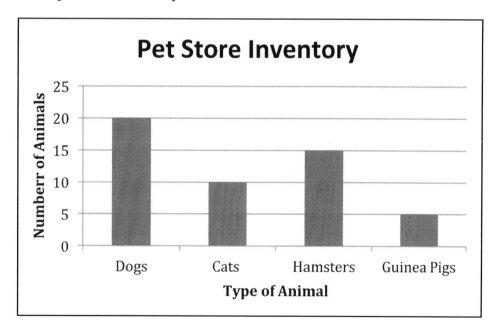

The owner of a small pet store performs an inventory of the animals in his store. The results are summarized in the bar graph above.

3. How many more dogs were in the pet store than guinea pigs?
    (A) 3
    (B) 5
    (C) 10
    (D) 15
    (E) 20

To answer this question, we have to figure out how many dogs and how many guinea pigs were in the store when the inventory was performed. If we look at the bar chart, we can see that there were 20 dogs in the store and 5 guinea pigs. Since it is a "how many more" question, we find the difference between 20 and 5, which is 15. Answer choice D is correct.

More complex bar graphs

One type of bar graph that you may see has bars that compare the same thing at different times.

Here is an example of how you may see this type of bar graph question on the SSAT:

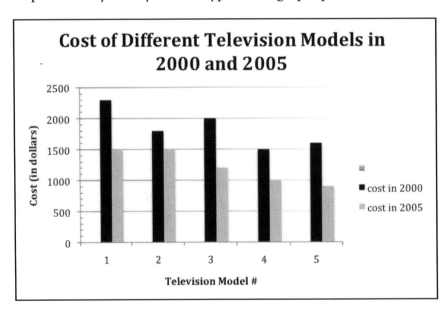

4. The original price of which model was reduced by one-third between 2000 and 2005?
    (A) Model #1
    (B) Model #2
    (C) Model #3
    (D) Model #4
    (E) Model #5

In order to solve this question, we have to multiply each of the model prices in 2000 by one-third and then subtract that from the price in 2000. The answer choice that gives us the 2005 value when we subtract one-third from the 2000 price is the correct answer. If we take the 2000 price ($1500) of Model #4 and multiply by one-third, we get that the price should be reduced by $500. If we reduce $1500 by $500, then we get $1000, which is the 2005 price of Model #4. This means that answer choice D is correct.

Here is another one to try using the same graph of television model prices:

5. The television model that cost the least in 2005 was what price in 2000?
    (A) $900
    (B) $1000
    (C) $1200
    (D) $1500
    (E) $1600

The trick to this question is just to keep track of the details. This is a multi-step problem. First we have to figure out which television model cost the least in 2005. Then we have to figure out what the same television cost in 2000. If we look at the gray bars, we can see that model #5 cost the least in 2005. If we look at the black bar for the same model, we can see that Model #5 cost $1600 in 2000, so answer choice E is correct.

Another type of bar graph that you may see breaks down the bars into fractional pieces.

Here is an example of how you might see this type of graph on the SSAT:

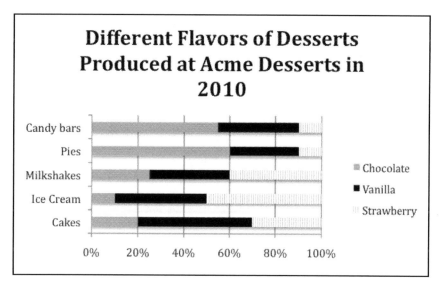

6. The fractional part of the cakes produced by Acme Desserts in 2010 that were vanilla was
    (A) ⅕
    (B) ³⁄₁₀
    (C) ½
    (D) ⁷⁄₁₀
    (E) ⅘

To solve this question, we first have to figure out what percent of the cakes produced were vanilla. The black bar represents vanilla cakes. It starts at 20% and then goes until 70%. If we find the difference between the two, we can see that 50% of the cakes produced were vanilla. Since 50% is equal to ½, answer choice C is correct.

Here is another one to try:

7. What fractional part of the milkshakes produced by Acme Desserts in 2010 was strawberry?
    (A) ⅕
    (B) ³⁄₁₀
    (C) ⅖
    (D) ⅗
    (E) ⁷⁄₁₀

If we look at the graph, we can see that the striped part of the bar for milkshakes (the striped portion represents strawberry milkshakes) takes up 40% of the bar. Another way to write 40% is $\frac{40}{100}$. If we reduce $\frac{40}{100}$ then we get $\frac{2}{5}$ and answer choice C is correct.

Circle graphs

Circle graph problems are relatively straightforward on the SSAT. Generally, these problems ask you to translate from a percent or fraction into a circle graph, or vice versa.

Here are the basic benchmarks that you should know

$\frac{1}{4} = 25\% =$

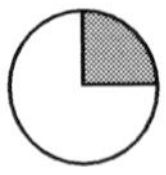

$\frac{1}{2} = 50\% =$

$\frac{3}{4} = 75\% =$

Here is an example of a problem like those you might see on the SSAT testing circle graphs:

8. Gregory wants to make a circle graph showing the percentage of tennis matches that he has won. This season, he has won 4 matches and lost 4 matches. Which circle graph shows this correctly?

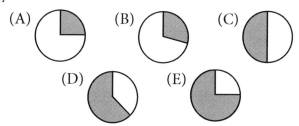

In order to answer this question, we first have to figure out what fraction or percent of his matches he won. Since he won 4 matches and lost 4 matches, he won half of his matches. Answer choice C correctly represents him winning half of his matches.

The best way to ace the graph questions is through practice. Be sure to complete the graphs practice set.

Graphs Practice Set

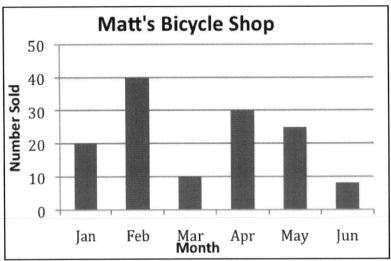

1. During which of the following two-month periods did Matt's Shop sell the most bicycles?
   (A) January and February
   (B) February and March
   (C) March and April
   (D) April and May
   (E) May and June

2. In August, ten fewer than twice the number of bikes sold in April were sold. How many bikes were sold in August?
   (A) 15
   (B) 25
   (C) 40
   (D) 50
   (E) 60

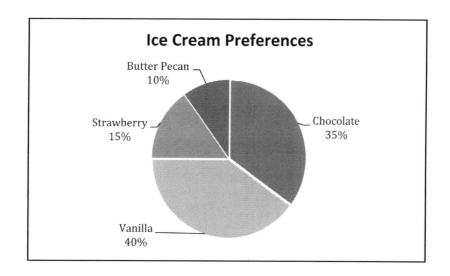

A total of 300 people were asked their favorite ice cream. The results are summarized in the circle graph.

3. How many people preferred chocolate ice cream?
    (A) 35
    (B) 45
    (C) 105
    (D) 120
    (E) Cannot be determined

4. How many more people preferred vanilla than butter pecan?
    (A) 30
    (B) 60
    (C) 90
    (D) 120
    (E) 150

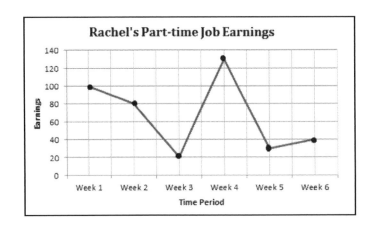

Rachel's Part-time Job Earnings

5. Rachel has a part-time job helping her neighbor with chores and errands. Each week she keeps track of her earnings, and the earnings for her first 6 weeks of work are displayed in the line graph. How much total money did Rachel earn in weeks 3 and 4?
   (A) $20
   (B) $65
   (C) $110
   (D) $120
   (E) $150

6. Comparing Rachel's Week 3 earnings to her week 2 earnings, we would say that
   (A) They are $\frac{1}{4}$ as much
   (B) They are $\frac{1}{3}$ as much
   (C) They are half as much
   (D) They are twice as much
   (E) They are four times as much

Answers to Graph Practice Set

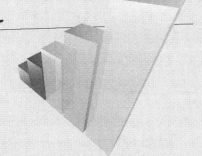

1. A
2. D
3. C
4. C
5. E
6. A

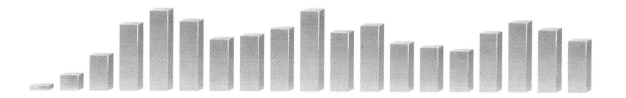

Tips For the Writing Sample

Please Note: The writing sample on the Middle Level SSAT was updated for the 2012-2013 testing season. The advice and information in this book is up to date, but books from other publishers may not have been updated yet, so do not be alarmed if the information in this book and others does not match. You can always check www.ssat.org if you have any questions since that is the official website of the SSATB.

When you take the SSAT, you will be asked to complete a writing sample. You will be given 25 minutes and two pages to write your response. Your writing sample will NOT be scored. Rather, a copy of it will be sent to the schools that you apply to.

With the recently redesigned writing sample, you will be given a choice between two creative writing prompts.

The creative prompts might look like "story starters" that a teacher may have used in your school. The test writers will give you a starting sentence and you take it from there.

Here are some examples of what these questions could look like:

- A strange wind blew through town on that Thursday night.
- He thought long and hard before slowly opening the door.
- She had never been in an experience quite like this before.

To approach the writing sample, follow this four step plan:

Step 1: Choose Topic

- Go with the prompt that creates a bigger "spark" in your mind

Step 2: Plan

- Take just a couple of minutes and plan, it will be time well spent

- Be sure to know what your problem is and how it will be resolved

Step 3: Write

- Break your writing into paragraphs- don't do a two page blob

- Remember to start new paragraphs for dialogue and to break up long descriptions

- Write legibly- it does not have to be perfect and schools know that you are writing with a time limit, but if the admissions officers can't read what you wrote, they can't judge it

Step 4: Edit/Proofread

- Save a couple of minutes for the end to look over your work

- You won't be able to do a major editing job where you move around sentences and rewrite portions

- Look for where you may have left out a word or misspelled something

- Make your marks simple and clear- if you need to take something out, just put a single line through it and use a carat to insert words that you forgot

The writing sample is not graded, but the schools that you apply to do receive a copy.

So what are schools looking for?

Organization

There should be structure to your story. There needs to be a problem, which builds to a climax, and then a resolution. Since you only have two pages and 25 minutes to get this done, you should know your problem before you begin to write. The biggest mistake that students make is not knowing their resolution before they begin to write. They can't drop clues as they write because they don't know where the story is going! What happens is that students write themselves into a corner and then have to do something that makes no sense in order to get their characters out of a real bind.

Word choice

Use descriptive language. Don't describe anything as "nice" or "good". Describe specifically why something is nice or good. Good writing shows us and DOESN'T tell us.

Creativity and development of ideas

It is not enough just to be able to fit your writing into the form that you were taught in school. These prompts are designed to show how you think. This is your chance to shine! With these creative prompts, this is your chance to come up with unique ideas.

The writing sample is a place for you to showcase your writing skills. It is just one more piece of information that the admissions committee will use in making their decisions.

52802693R00164

Made in the USA
Lexington, KY
10 June 2016